Your Church:
A DYNAMIC COMMUNITY

Your Church:
A DYNAMIC
COMMUNITY

Arleon L. Kelley

The Westminster Press
Philadelphia

Book Design by Alice Derr

First edition

Published by The Westminster Press®
Philadelphia, Pennsylvania

PRINTED IN THE UNITED STATES OF AMERICA
9 8 7 6 5 4 3 2 1

Library of Congress Cataloging in Publication Data

Kelley, Arleon L. (Arleon Leigh), 1935–
   Your church.

    1. Church. 2. Sociology, Christian.
I. Title.
BV600.2.K4   254   81–23159
ISBN 0–664–24411–4   AACR2

Contents

Preface

THIS BOOK GROWS out of a lifelong concern with the church as a human community. My experience repeatedly has been enriched and challenged by confrontation with change in church groups—from local parishes to regional and national organizations.

The ideas in this book have been stimulated through work with professional colleagues. A variety of persons have assisted in the clarification of my thinking. The Roman Catholic–Reformed Churches Bilateral Dialogues on "The Shape of the Unity We Seek" was one important forum of discussion. Another was the development of an article with Martha Miller, executive director of the Dutchess (County in New York) Interfaith Council on "The Theology of Organization" for publication in the Living Ecumenism Series. I am indebted to fellow participants in a state faith and order conference; staff colleagues at the National Council of the Churches of Christ in the U.S.A. and the NCCC's Governing Board Panel on "The Nature of Ecumenical Commitment and the NCCC's Purposes," chaired by Paul A. Crow, Jr. These persons have all contributed richly to insights and thinking about the church as an organization in society.

Finally, I am grateful for the understanding and patience of Jackie, my wife, and the assistance of colleagues Margaret Duffy and Noemi Garcia in preparing the manuscripts to make the completion of this book possible.

A.L.K.

Chapter I

COMMUNITY

GOD SEEKS TO FULFILL creation through the church. The church is important in carrying out God's intentions. However, Christian people are not always conscious of the church as a human community, whose purposes and ways of acting may vary greatly. Yet as a human group, the Christian church has always needed to choose among alternatives, in self-definition and mission.

In the early period Peter and Paul advocated different options for the church as an organization. Peter maintained that only people who first became Jews could become Christians, while Paul argued that the requirements were only belief in Christ and baptism. Peter's alternative, from an organizational standpoint, would have caused the Christian church to remain a subdivision of Judaism. But Paul prevailed and transformed the dynamic message of Jesus by interpreting it in Greek and Roman cultural symbolism that made it understandable to those outside the Jewish faith. With the inclusion of pagan members, Christianity became a religion of broader appeal that developed an organizational style in harmony with the cultural milieu of the Greco-Roman world.

The church in various periods has developed organizational systems that both reflect and speak to contemporary conditions. The Roman Catholic Church, for example, in its organizational style shows the influence of the later Roman Empire. During the Reformation, the organization of the Lutheran church, particularly in Germany, emerged from the subdivisions of the country and followed the development toward national unification. At the same time, the organizational style of groups like the Mennonites, and some Baptists, grew from the life of separatists, who were the individualists of their day, resulting in a democratic congregational style. Similarly, the Reformed churches reflect the style of representative democracy that was developing during the time of their formation. The following contemporary examples illustrate the variety of organizational dynamics in modern churches, both at the parish level and, even more broadly, as they seek to fulfill their roles as a community.

In a large county-seat town, a congregation was alive and vital. The sanctuary was filled for services twice each Sunday morning. The church school was growing, there were a hundred and twenty young people in the Sunday evening youth programs, Bible study groups were well attended, young people were deciding to be missionaries and ministers, and the church gave one dollar for others for each dollar it spent on itself. The church was the moral leader of its community. To be a part of such a vital fellowship could not be mistaken for anything other than a vital witness of God's love to the whole community. This church showed God's intention that people live in whole and redemptive relationships.

Yet the experience of such a church is exceptional.

In contrast is another parish comprised of eleven rural churches. Although the members of those churches were committed Christians, their churches expressed little vitality. One small congregation in that parish had nineteen members, predominantly older, retired people. The congregation was located in a community burgeoning with

children, but none of them attended the church school in
that church. A new pastor began calling door to door in
the community to meet the parents of these children. At
the end of a visit, he would invite the parents to bring their
children to the church school. Almost as if in refrain, the
parents would refuse because they felt they would seem
different and unwelcome. Yet they would send their children on a church bus to a different, more remote church.

Another type of congregation developed successfully in
northeastern Ohio. The minister had come to the area
more than twenty years before from one of the Appalachian states. He gathered around himself a congregation
of people of similar background—most had immigrated to
that area during World War II and immediately following.
They had come for economic reasons, but they felt alienated from the dominant urban industrial culture. This
alienation became a means of rallying these people around
the minister. The congregation began to dream of having
the biggest cathedral in the area, with the most compre-
hensive television ministry in the country, and of sharing
worldwide the Christian message. This dream motivated
the people to action. They developed a membership of
thousands and had a television ministry in many cities of
the United States and Canada. They utilized some of their
resources to invest in other ventures, including a small
college. By all standards of organizational growth, num-
bers, and money, they seemed to be tremendously successful. Yet their success had little positive influence on
the development of their local community even though it
seemed to speak religiously across the nation to a certain
type of people. How were they able to focus such energy
and resources along some lines? How could they be so
influential religiously, yet not influence socially their immediate community? What was the relationship between
religious values and the organizational nature of the group
that caused this phenomenon?

In an urban neighborhood adjoining a large university, nearly all the established congregations were dying. The old middle-class residents had given way to Hispanic and Appalachian cultural groups. Neither was attracted to the religious life-style of these churches. Yet these congregations tried to survive by linking themselves with one another so they could more efficiently utilize their limited resources. Apart from some social ministries, their influence on the religious and neighborhood life was limited. Simultaneously, a group of charismatic Christians flourished in the same neighborhood and were related in one way or another to the university, either as professors, employees, or students. This group glowed with enthusiasm and zeal, while at the same time caring for one another. They shared what they had with one another and with others in the community who had unfilled needs. The quality of their existence was markedly different from that of persons in the more traditional congregations in that neighborhood. Why did the organized congregations seem to struggle for mere organizational survival, while this cluster of forty to fifty charismatics thrived and exhibited so much care for one another and for their fellow human beings outside the group? Why were the charismatics relating so creatively to the surrounding community while those in the congregation were having so much difficulty relating to that same community?

Many congregations in both rural America and the inner city have long since lost their sense of mission. Because of this inertia, many Christians who expect community effectiveness from the church have developed an anti-institutional bias. In the late 1960s and early 1970s many persons left their churches, having seen the way institutions can absorb money and energy as a pillow absorbs the blow of a fist without ever a feather flying. These people realized that for all the resources used, there was little resulting influence by their congregations either on the surrounding community or in their own lives. Because of this observation about many churches as well as other community organizations, "movement people" avoided formal organizations or institutions. Rather, they built temporary task forces, coalitions, committees, or collaborating groups to perform a single job. After completion of the job, they disbanded to go on to perform some other task in a different coalitional configuration. This phenomenon has resulted in an anti-institutional bias that has caused thousands of once viable congregations and several hundred former ecumenical councils of churches as well as other organizations to be systematically dissolved. In a majority of the cases, these church and church-related organizations were not replaced by new and more flexible organizations, and the broader community needs went unmet. When the older organizations were phased out, not enough energy could be focused to create new ones. Experiences with this variety of church groups lead to a number of premises fundamental to this book.

The church, while acting for God, also reflects its human environment. Clearly the church can be understood as a human organization, a group of people who have a continuing life together, whether only a few, as in some local congregations, or whether as a denomination on a national or international level, or whether as part of the church throughout time. The total church comprises many constituent groups or organizations with different organizational styles, including governance, ways of interacting, and mission or values. Nonreligious organizations may vary in similar ways, but the church is unique in its role of carrying forward God's intentions for the fulfillment of all of creation. God entrusts the church to further the creative process of bringing order and wholeness out of chaos or disparity. Creative energy is precious and may be rare. However, moments of greatness in the history of the church as a human community have occurred with the creative transformation of a religious insight into values which are shared by people who then constitute a group of believers. At a later stage, when enthusiasm begins to lag, community renewal occurs when a few creative people are able to redefine these values in the chaos of changing conditions. To some degree these patterns hold true of all human organizations, but the churches' values have to do with ultimate realities and basic meaning. The church holds organized systems of belief and practices to help both members and those outside the church to live in harmony with these ultimate realities. The mission of the church, whether local or universal, is not just to nurture religious values and faith, but to work to actualize these values by participating in God's ongoing creative process, by manifesting wholeness, and by serving the entire human community. The church is to be a prototype community pointing to the possibility of and hope for creation's fulfillment.

Chapter II

PURPOSE

VISITS TO THE WORK PLACES of John Calvin in Geneva, John Wesley in London, Peter Waldo in Italy, Roger Williams in Rhode Island, and Thomas and Alexander Campbell in West Virginia can remind one how these reformers led to the organization of great streams of Christian practice in the church. Even more ancient sites in Jerusalem, Galilee, Damascus, Greece, Egypt, and Rome— great centers of the ancient world—bring to mind how our forebears influenced the images and the story of our faith. In the latter places the organization we know as the church was born and grew into a vital witness in the cultural world of the Romans. In the case of the reformers, new insights about God's intention for the church were developed. Then, through organization, these insights contributed to a more effective and renewed church. These great leaders not only were able to develop new insights about the relationship of Creator to the creation, they were also able to give an organizational form to that creative new insight so that the ideas could have a lasting impact upon the developing church as well as upon society.

What is true in the church is also true in other parts of society. The founders of the United States used ideas about social contracts, human liberty, and balance among the legislative, administrative, and judicial functions of government that were advanced for their time. Others had thought similar thoughts before them, yet in contrast these founders were able to give their creative dreams and ideas organizational form—form that translated those insights into a working structure meeting human needs.

These historic experiences raise the basic question: Why is the casting of a religious, political, or economic idea into organized form so important? Organization translates ideas into a reality that people can understand. An idea is focused energy possessed by one or a few persons. In order to have coinage in the marketplace it must be given symbolism so it can be communicated and organizational form so its energy and impact can be multiplied rather than dissipated. Organization disciplines an idea in the sense that it keeps all who share the idea "pulling" in the same direction. Conversely, people concerned for individual freedom often distrust groups, particularly beyond the local community, because they do put demands on them as persons. The irony is that this tendency, if shared by the majority, would create chaos, if not anarchy. Society would be unable to fulfill humankind's most fundamental needs. What, then, are the alternatives? Why do we have organizations? Why do they serve us well at some times in our history, and at other times in our history why do they function to oppress us?

There are both sociological factors and theological factors that point to possible answers to these questions. First, the sociological: organizations arise as a means whereby persons through cooperation can meet their basic human needs. These needs, which will be discussed in detail later, can be summarized as relating either to survival or to fulfillment.

In its simplest form, an organization is a cooperative compromise or trade-off between two persons so that the needs of each might be more fully realized. For example, if

I have proficiency in picking berries and finding vegetables, and you have proficiency in hunting and providing meat, it may well be that you and I will strike an agreement that I will provide berries and vegetables for you if you will provide meat for me. Both of us benefit by having a more adequate diet. Eventually, other people may enter into the agreement with us so that one person is providing milk and cheese, while still another person contributes fish. In this manner, everyone's diet is enhanced. In the simple tribal society, the organization for sharing food did not go much beyond this. Yet in a more complex society, other parties soon enter into the organizational chain: a farmer, a miller, a baker. In still more complex societies the same chain might be a grain elevator operator between the farmer and the miller and a retail store between the baker and the customer. This same cycle might also evolve with producers of vegetables in need of markets and producers of meat in need of markets. Thus, a simple agreement that enabled two persons to meet their varied needs for food evolves into a very complex economic structure. The complex economic structure made it possible for efficiency to increase, up to a certain point, and for people to have a greater variety of choices of food they could eat.

A similar model might be developed to describe how religious organizations have arisen. As people were learning to meet the most fundamental day-to-day needs for food and shelter, their minds were also wondering about the world, and more particularly, its aspects that were not understood. Where did we come from? Why did my father die? Why did my friend's child die? What are the causes of hurricanes, lightning, fires, and floods? Can people control these mighty forces of nature that seem to bring so much harm to life?

Subsequently, the need arose to pass their insights about the world on to their children. People—in groups of two, four, twenty, or thirty persons—developed patterned answers to questions. Some surmised from their experience that every object, whether animate or inanimate, possessed life. This particular kind of thinking, called animism, developed a whole explanation of the universe that grew from the assumption that all objects possessed life. Animists called out from their number one or more persons whose task it was both to reflect upon the group's accumulated knowledge and to teach the children in the society about this knowledge. The selected person or persons also helped the community to enter into dramatic ceremonies that would appease the living spirits and thus control the forces of nature.

Over a long period of time, as humankind interacted with its environment, it built ever more sophisticated understandings about humankind's relationship with the creation. This was passed on to later generations as accumulated wisdom. It was also passed on as folklore through symbols, tales, and ceremonies. The ceremonial practices celebrating the garnered wisdom became a fundamental means for humankind to deal with the most basic questions of life. Those interacting forces are the basis for religion, where the people for whom these ideas and practices are important form organizations as a means of nurturing their understanding and transmitting their understandings to others.

Similar sociological descriptions can be developed for the rise of the basic institutions in our society, including the clan or tribe, as well as the economic institutions, political institutions, and educational institutions.

Organizational life can also be explained in terms of level of complexity or sphere of influence. The simplest form is the relationship between two persons cooperating to meet their fundamental needs. The second sphere in complexity is the informal organization—defined as two or more persons cooperating together to meet their needs through mutual agreements. The third sphere of complexity is the more formal institution. Here formal contracts are devised to guide the behavior of the participants in that organization as well as providing a means for them to train their progeny in the values to be derived from that organization. These more formal institutions encouraged a further rise to a fourth level of sophistication. This sphere develops from alliances among similar institutions with all of the symbolic language and professional trappings that go along with this level of sophistication. When all the systems described in the fourth sphere interact, they produce a dominant cultural pattern, such as European culture, American culture, or African culture. These cultures in turn interact with one another to produce dominant civilization patterns, such as Western civilization or Eastern civilization. The patterns of a dominant civilization are the most extensive sphere of organizational complexity. Thus, sociological description of organizations not only involves their nature—i.e., economic, religious, or political—but also includes spheres of influence or of complexity.

People live in social arrangements so each person may be fulfilled to the maximum. These arrangements exist precisely in order that people, through mutual help, cooperation, and division of labor, may fulfill themselves better than if they lived apart. But still, describing organizations from a sociological perspective only begins to tell what an organization is and why it functions as it does. Thus, the task of describing organizations is incomplete. One knows that organizations emerge to meet the needs of humankind. But what is it about God's creation that makes organization the best way to meet human needs? Therefore, theological reflection becomes an essential means to gain understanding of the questions about what an organization is and why it exists.

This gives rise to the second premise, which is that the need for organization is rooted in the nature of God's creation itself. Basically, organizations help humankind to order its life. But why, and toward what end, is it ordering its life? What is there about creation that makes it necessary for humankind to order its life, and even beyond, for it to seek survival, self-fulfillment, and the answering of some of the more basic questions of life? What about the survival of humankind if mortal individuals will not survive? Is there something greater than us as individuals toward which we are striving and working?

The answers to these and other questions would seem to lie in the basic meaning of the nature of the Creator, the creation, and humankind. God's creation may be considered the objective manifestation of the Creator's intentionality. In the first chapter of Genesis, the Creator began a process of bringing order out of void or chaos. The ordering was just that, a process. Slowly and gradually, the chaos of the void was ordered into the reality known as the cosmos, or universe. Most scientists now believe that the universe did in fact go through a birth process which in effect caused the countless stars to be. Within each of these stars, like our sun, mighty forces were at work. From the primordial atoms a process of ever-increasing complexity began—much more like a developing great idea than a static system. Over a great period of time, as the creation developed, the conditions were right for humankind to come into existence. But with the origin of humankind, creation was not yet fulfilled. In humankind God had made a being to act as co-creator, endowed with characteristics not unlike God's—i.e., with creativity, consciousness of being different from other parts of the creation and yearning to see the process of creation fulfilled. This reality is indicated in the letter to the Romans: "The created universe waits with eager expectation for God's sons to be revealed. . . . The universe itself is to be freed from the shackles of mortality. . . . The whole created universe groans in all its parts as if in the pangs of childbirth" (Rom. 8:19ff., NEB).

The two creation accounts of Genesis, when compared with the fulfillment images of Revelation, give clear clues to the creation's intended direction. Specifically, the first creation story (Gen. 1:1 to 2:4) begins with void—darkness, nothingness—and then describes the process of ordering which makes it possible for animals and humankind to emerge on the fifth day or phase of creation. In this phase humankind's purpose was made clear: "Be fruitful, increase, fill the earth, be in charge." In other words, be the steward of the created order.

In the second creation account of Genesis (2:4ff.), the initial image is of barrenness. Then came the water in the form of a flood, which created the conditions for life. Here God formed humankind and created a garden with rivers flowing through it as the continuing source of life. God told humankind to cultivate the garden and care for it.

In both creation stories there is progression from lifelessness to life. Humankind is given the role of caring for and participating in the ongoing ordering and creation. The nature and struggle of that participation becomes the central theme of the Bible. The nature of the task is aptly described in a variety of ways, particularly as the hope toward which we are to strive. The image of that struggle for hope and expectation is spelled out in the struggles of Israel; in God's covenants with Israel; in the visions of Ezekiel and Daniel and other prophets; in the new covenant when God dramatized the ongoing intention for creation; in the incarnation, death, and resurrection of Jesus; and is expressed finally in the Revelation of John, the vision of creation's fulfillment. Biblically, creation begins with a desert that flowers into a garden and it ends with a transfigured city with a garden in its midst. It is a movement from lifelessness to life, and from nothingness to complexity.

Creation is thus depicted as a continuing and directional phenomenon moving toward fulfillment, with humankind

playing a unique role in the development. We are created
in the image of the Creator, whose principal attribute is
ongoing creativity—continuing involvement in the creative process.

In the Old Testament, the dynamic creative intentionality of the Creator is identified by leading Hebrew scholars
as the spirit embodied in "Torah." In the New Testament,
this creativity is embodied in the concept "Word." This
continuing creative force brings wholeness or atonement
in its literal sense of being "at one" with the creative
process. "Torah" and "Word" symbolize the creative idea
from which the created universe is given form and dyna-
mism. Therefore, both the Old Testament and the New
Testament become witnesses that humankind is called to
join with the Creator in this ongoing creative process—
i.e., to affirm the Torah and the Word, and to become
co-creators or participants in the process of moving the
creation toward its fulfillment. As Jewish theological wisdom says, we are dependent upon God and God depends
upon us—interdependence in the creative process. This is
what it means to be created in God's image. This implies
that each person has the capability of working intention-
ally with the Creator to move the creation toward fulfillment. We are essential to the fulfillment of God's purpose,
and through creation to the fulfillment of God! Yet humankind, like God, has the power of choice. This is not true for
other creatures. We can choose not to be "at one" with the
Creator in the ongoing creation, or we can choose to oppose the development of creation, anticreatively—one understanding of the meaning of sin. Anticreation or sin may
be defined as anything humankind does personally or in
groups that pushes the creation back toward the chaos
from whence it came. A dynamic creation, moving toward
fulfillment, is developing toward goals set by God. Attempts to stop this motion by affirmation of a static, rigid
status quo become anticreative acts, because they try to

stop progress at one temporary stage of development. Therefore, relatively speaking, to affirm the status quo while the rest of creation goes on, is, in fact, to lose ground —to push the creation back toward the chaos from which it came.

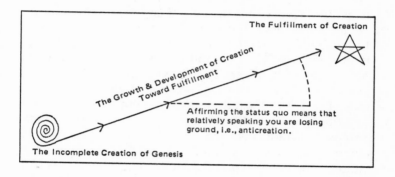

Put another way, if the creation is moving on a tangent toward fulfillment on a forty-five-degree angle, the status quo is represented as an attempt to interrupt the process by leveling out or stopping it. If the past is affirmed in the present, then, relatively speaking, the status quo is getting out of touch with the realities of creation. Therefore, the status quo, when related to the direction of ongoing history, tends to be pushing the creation back toward the chaos in which it originated.

The ordering or organizing of human activity is one of the principal ways in which humankind participates in the ongoing creative process. It is the means by which human life is ordered for creative interaction with the rest of creation. Organization, functioning properly, is the dimension that frees humankind from chaos with its destructive and anticreative results. Organization can facilitate the possibility of human fulfillment within the dimensions of creation.

This creative freedom is always difficult for humankind to accept. Human creativity in a social context is difficult at best, and terrifying at worst. The status quo is more comfortable, at least initially.

In religious history, an unwillingness to follow a creative path is repeated time and time again. For example, the Israelites moved from the collegiality represented by the judges to a more traditional kingship, as recorded in I Samuel 8. Here is shown the common human temptation to give up creative freedom to others, who then use it to put people in bondage. People who are oppressed often participate in their own oppression. Liberation, on the other hand, is deliberate participation in creative change regardless of adversity. This, then, becomes the foundation for our understanding the unique role of the church among the constellation of human organizations. The church is to be a prototype organization. This means that the church as a people, as an organization, and as the embodiment of the Word exists to demonstrate creative alternatives and liberating possibilities. If this is true, then the church as an organization is qualitatively different from other parts of societal organization. The church should be no less than the embodiment of the dynamic idea which is the essence of creation. It is to be the embodiment of Torah and Word. The church is called to be the prototype of whole and redemptive group relationships demonstrating to the other organizations in the society their possibility also of being redemptive, creative communities in the dimensions of time and space. The church is the dramatization of God's purposes in creation. It is the sign and symbol that dramatizes God's intention for organizations. It embodies creativity, community, and wholeness, the three attributes of fulfillment. These dramatize for humankind both God's intention for creation and the possibilities that are inherent in human existence.

Chapter III

TIME

YESTERDAY'S CREATIVITY is often today's obstacle to progress. What difference does time make? Near the downtown area of a city in New England, one large church building was an impressive monument to that congregation's importance in an earlier era of community vitality. This was the church of the supervisors, technicians, and workers who had been instrumental in making the lace and textile mills of that city so profitable in the nineteenth and the early twentieth century. Through their church participation the members were fulfilled and were also able to make a contribution to the community.

Yet, recently, the congregation had been undergoing a slow and painful decline—a decline explained in part by the shifting economic fortunes of the city, and also in part by the influx of immigrants who were mostly Roman Catholic. Consequently, the participants in that Protestant congregation were largely older adults whose children long since either had left the community or had married Catholics and had promised to raise their children in the Catholic Church. The church provided a valuable service in visitation to shut-ins and the ill, as well as conducting an average of three funerals a week, but it had few baptisms and marriages, and little in the way of children's church school or youth ministry.

With few Protestants in the community; with decline, decay, and hopelessness all around; and with a congregation of older adults, the prognosis was bleak. There were not enough resources in the church to maintain and heat the building, while at the same time maintaining the pastor at minimum salary. The church had reached a stage of crisis.

Although there is a creative sequel concerning what eventually happened with this congregation, the concern at this point is to explore the underlying dynamics or processes that caused this congregation's predicament. The forces at work in this church affect all organizations. What are the processes that make a church or any other organization creative at one time and less than creative at another time? The answers have much to do with time and the processes of development as well as with the interaction with the broader community situation.

TRANSCENDENCE AND TIME

History and time are conceived as crucial to understanding the purpose of organizations. From the very dawning of human consciousness, people have been concerned about time and history. Time was one of the first abstract ideas to be quantified in human social history. There are indications that at the very earliest times in history, people had worked out rather sophisticated calendars with divisions such as days, weeks, months, and years.

It is also quite evident from anthropological data that even the earliest human beings kept some records of their past. This was done in at least three ways. Folk tales were shared around the campfire as one means of perpetuating the memory of what they had been as a group of persons. Another way that records were kept was through the artifacts that each successive generation of tribal life left behind. These included the implements and tools utilized for day-to-day life. They also included the artwork left on cave walls as well as the rather elaborate and exquisite carvings on temples, in caves, and on buildings.

Philosophical understandings of time have varied. When the major Eastern and Western philosophers were emerging on the scene, some six hundred years before the common era (B.C.E.), time was perceived by some as an alternating rhythm. Some Chinese related this to Yang and Yin. Yang represented the areas of aggressive cultural development and was seen as the male force in history. Yin represented the passive periods and the female forces in history. Empedocles, the Greek philosopher, had a similar view which he called periods of "strife" (roughly analogous to the Chinese Yang), and periods of "love" (analogous to the Yin concept in Chinese literature). Both tended to believe that when either principle went to an extreme, it lopped over into the other principle. Thus, extreme Yin or love would produce Yang or strife, and vice versa.

More contemporary philosophers have tended to view time in still another fashion. Philosophers of "process" have tended to believe that people move from a fixed past into the unfolding future. In this view, change is real and history is seen as developmental. On the other hand, other philosophers maintained that past, future, and present all exist at the same time. What people are currently experiencing and believe to be a movement or flow of time is an illusion. There is no real change. Change is an illusion. These views significantly affect perspectives of organizational life.

The Christian tradition has had elements of both of these concepts. Sometimes it has held that persons function from choice, and those choices affect the future. Change is real. Those who have affirmed the concept of predestination or election would find some affinity with the other view. It is similar to the argument that past, present, and future all exist and therefore the response of the individual (election) is given from birth. The sociologist Max Weber observed that, strangely, even though the latter concept should have apparently worked against active organization and activism in history, it has had quite the opposite effect. He argued that in order for people to prove that they were among the elect and therefore among the blessed, they engaged in hyperactivity which led to some of the most sophisticated and complex societal organization known to humankind. He argues that ideas of predestination, although they may have been misunderstood, were causal in the rise of the industrialized, activist, and expansionary culture of the West.

The fact would seem to be that both perspectives have been acted out in a similar fashion and developed a common middle ground.

The concept of eschatology as developed by most Christian traditions is a theological idea also related to the philosophy of time. Essentially, it is an argument that time has a beginning and an end—it is created and it will come to fulfillment. Initially, this idea would seem to argue for a straight-line flow of time or the theory that history is directional. Simply put, Christian theology has tended to view time and history in two ways, neither unique to the experience of any particular Christian theological formulation. Some have thought that history would lead to greater and greater chaos or sin, and the eschatological event would be the divine intervention that would pluck the holy out of the chaos, and then destroy the chaos or let the chaos destroy itself. Others have viewed time, history, and the eschatological event more optimistically. They have seen history as moving toward greater and greater wholeness, until such time as the creation is completed. This view sees a purpose to history and creation. It is a process of bringing order or wholeness out of chaos. The eschatological event is therefore seen as that time of fulfillment when the creation and the Creator are in harmony, at-one-ment, with each other.

There is some truth in both views. God can intervene in human history, as in the life of Jesus. Through this incarnation God's intention for creation's fulfillment is clear. Yet, in general, God has self-limited creative power by bringing humankind into a co-creative relationship. If there is true interdependence between God and people, humankind could fail. The covenant stories have long indicated God's constancy in relationship and humankind's propensity for unfaithfulness. Yet, if there was not the latter possibility, humankind would be less than human—only a puppet in the Creator's scheme.

An optimistic view about humankind's role in creation's fulfillment provides a basis for understanding the nature of, and the need for, organizational growth and development among the human sectors of creation. The thesis of this book emerges from this perspective. It is that human interaction produces organization, and through organization humankind participates in the dimensions of history. If humankind is to have worth and purpose in the creation, organization must provide means for participation in that creation.

The human experience would seem to argue for this, because at the same time that people have been very concerned about their past, they have also been very concerned about their future. If there is no hope for fulfillment in the creation, why the concern? What is the basis of hope? If there is evidence in the very earliest recorded knowledge that humankind was concerned for the future, why? One very obvious reason had to do with the understandings that persons had of their own finiteness. If life was to have meaning, many felt there must be something beyond the present circumstances and something beyond death. If there was nothing, then life apparently is folly. There is evidence in many of our cultures and civilizations, both past and present, of great preoccupation with the future. For example, the Jews perceived they were the chosen people. Why were they so chosen if there was no hope for the future? Nearly all civilizations have some cultural theme that represents a hope of that civilization being translated into some future fulfilled state of existence. In the Christian tradition, this hope sometimes has to do with the second coming of Christ—the Apocalypse. These predominant cultural themes would seem to argue for the validity of a past, present, and future view of history, as opposed to the purely existential view. Anthropology would seem to substantiate a developmental view of that history, at least in terms of sophistication if not in terms of quality.

Yet the concepts of past, present, and future would seem to be inextricably related to the concept of the ongoing process of creation toward fulfillment. This is becoming more evident in some of the contemporary scientific hypotheses about the nature of time and space. Past, present, and future are "now" in a very real sense. We are the product of all that is past. We live in the existential moment, but we do so in hope of the future.

Many theologians, such as Karl Barth, have argued that the people of God transcend time, i.e., all those who are in harmony, at-one-ment, with the purposes of the Creator and the creation in the present are standing, arms intertwined, with all those who had preceded them in faith commitment as well as with all those who would follow them in that faith. Thus, creative participation in the ongoing creation has long been seen theologically as transcending the dimensions of time. This is to say that all the people of God are participants in the truest sense, and not only in the past and the present but also in the future. They are creatures of the past, living today in the hope of the future. Past, present, and future are one, but in a different sense from that argued by the philosophers. Creation had a beginning and will be fulfilled. To be a participant in the purposes of creation transcends time, in the sense that time and space are one, i.e., history and creation are one.

Organizations play a very important role in humankind's participation in past, present, and future. Organizations are like an ongoing cosmic, oscillating current, which is not unlike the Yang and Yin of Chinese philosophy. Organizations are created by humankind to maintain contact with the past in the dimensions of time and space. Through organization the past human dimensions of creation can be related for either creative or oppressive participation in the present as well as providing the means through which to participate in our hopes and dreams for the future. Organizations are seen as oscillating because they have high points of creativity and low troughs of rigidity that impede creativity. They also transcend time in the sense that no viable organization exists without embodying hopes, dreams, and aspirations of people. These dimensions which relate to the future are the fundamental organizing principles for an organization. In other words, an organization is a device which makes it possible for people to move together toward the fulfillment of their needs, hopes, aspirations, and dreams. In a sense, it is a means helping them transcend time, because through organizations it is possible for the accumulated wisdom of previous generations to be utilized by current generations. It is a depository, if you will, of past accumulated wisdom. Through the nurturing function of an organization, that wisdom is transmitted to the next generation of participants along with the hopes and dreams of the current participants.

Thus, an organization is a means by which humankind can transcend the dimensions of past, present, and future. It utilizes the past and makes it possible to function in the present because it embodies the aspirations and hopes for the future. An organization is a means by which persons from the past and today have focused and are focusing their energy for participation in the ongoing creation.

If an organization is functioning up to its potential and purpose, there should be directional change involved in that organization's life. The Christian understanding of history is one of hope. The hope lies in the faith that creation is a continuing process moving from the chaos of undisciplined energy and material toward the fulfillment of creation. Fulfillment's principal characteristic will be manifested in bringing disciplined unity out of diversity. In other words, if chaos is defined as the aimless and chaotic wandering of the diverse parts of the primordial stuff, then fulfillment must mean that all parts of the diversity comprising that primordial stuff are now functioning in a totally complementary fashion that results in unity and wholeness of purposes—thus fulfilling creation. It is through organizations that humankind, although perhaps only a miniscule part of the creation, is privileged to be a participant in the creation process.

ORGANIZATIONS IN TERMS OF SOCIAL HISTORY

Organizations are intricately related to social history, which by definition is the story of the development of people, groups, and nations. It chronicles the developmental changes of organizations and civilizations. Organizational life is dynamic. If we are to believe that creation is in process, this would imply the development of social history. Change, either positive or negative, becomes normative. The social history of any given tribe or group of persons is influenced by a number of factors. Among them are: (a) the social context—where the organization finds itself in the overall development of social history; (b) allocated time—the values of the group and how the group allocates its available time out of each day, week, month, year, and generation; (c) technology—the ability to develop useful patterns of interaction between the human resources and the material resources at the group's command, patterns of interaction which in turn multiply the ability of humankind to interact further with the material at hand; (d) the environment, which includes many components, among which are the raw materials, the topography of the land, the climate, and the social milieu; and (e) finally, the people themselves—this includes the number of persons as well as the psychic climate which they create, the complexity of the organization which they develop, and their ability to respond to the other four factors.

Arnold Toynbee in studying the evolution of the earth's civilizations indicated that there are certain common characteristics of growth and decline that are true of organizations. After a phase of growth, each then enters into a phase called the "golden mean," a time of maximal effectiveness. And finally, his theory suggests that each experiences decline. This general pattern might be graphed in the following manner:

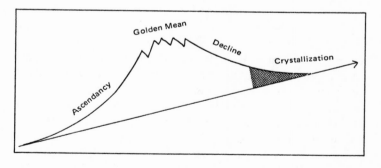

Concerning the forces that affect this life cycle of civilizations—the most complex of human organizations—

Toynbee develops two important ideas. One is that the civilization develops by responding creatively to significant challenges or problems. Another is the different ways in which creativity emerges. It is common in the stage of growth. During the time of the "golden mean," challenges are adequate to maintain creativity in a dominant majority of people. When this period ends, challenges become either too great or too inconsequential for the dominant majority. The society crystallizes and conducts "business as usual," while creativity is lodged primarily in a minority.

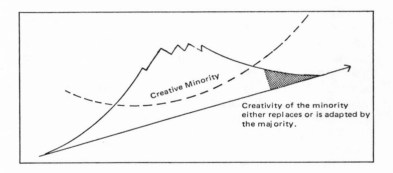

Creativity of the minority either replaces or is adapted by the majority.

In some cases, their creativity might be utilized by the dominant majority to make adjustments and modifications in a society that will continue to make it viable. On other occasions, however, the dominant majority may reject the creativity of the minority. If this happens in civilizations, two other results may occur, both of which are destructive of the dominant culture. One is that the majority may be overrun by outside masses of less-developed peoples, which in turn may replace a highly evolved society with a much less sophisticated society. Yet Toynbee argues even so for progress: the new society would be at least one step higher in its sophistication than the original form of society that it was replacing.

The other possibility is that the creative minority will, in fact, replace the old majority, and therefore create a whole new level in the development of that society or culture. These two possibilities could be diagrammed as shown on p. 34.

Therefore, social history can be seen as an evolutionary trend varying between ascending creativity and descending crystallization, but nonetheless pursuing an overall direction of increased sophistication. Environment, technology, time, organizational sophistication, and the creativity of the people themselves determine, to a large extent, the development of societies and organizations as well.

CREATIVITY AND SIN

One of the basic doctrines of the church deals with the concept of sin. How does this doctrine relate to an understanding of the rise and fall of organizations? The mythic theological basis for this concept has to do with the "fall in the Garden of Eden." The fall was humankind's means of describing the fundamental separation that humankind felt from the total purposes of creation —i.e., the lack of feeling at-one-ment with the creation. It is described in Genesis as an individual act of rebellion against the Creator and trying to put oneself in the Creator's place—being independent rather than interdependent. In the story of the wandering in the desert after escaping from Egypt, it is described as a whole society's unfaithfulness to the purposes of creation. It is again described in a similar fashion in the rebellion that led to the Babylonian captivity. Whether described individually or corporately, the concept of sin relates to an unfaithfulness to the best purposes which the Creator intends for humankind.

In the more contemporary traditions of the church, especially since the Reformation, sin has been perceived predominantly as a personal act which does not fit into what the religious group expects. Sometimes it is defined as deviation from the expectations of the whole society. At its worst, sin has been defined as a list of "don'ts." Defining it in this way has at least two results. First of all, it is dehumanizing because it does not give humankind credit for the ability to think creatively about involvement in the total creation. The person becomes a robot unable to reach the fullness of the potential involved in being human. Secondly, to define sin in this fashion also means being unable to deal with sin associated with groups. This has led to a dichotomy between personal morality and group responsibility. It was assumed that as long as the individual lives a moral life and does not engage in certain activities, society will function in a moral fashion as well. For example, the president of a large corporation could live a moral life by either religious or societal definition, while at the same time leading the corporation in making decisions that might harm or dehumanize the lives of thousands of persons.

It has been said that behind every great fortune lies a great social injustice. Frequently millions were made because employees did not receive their fair share of compensation from the gains of a particular corporation. Therefore, owners profited at the expense of the employees. This injustice can be defined as corporate sin. Another way of describing this would be to call these activities anticreative in the sense that they denied certain segments of humanity their just due. Ultimately, when organizations function in this manner, they become anticreative. They destroy their possibilities of contributing creatively.

Congregations as groups can also participate in anticreation in a similar fashion. One congregation's ministry was primarily to the individual person. Its understood purpose was to win persons for Christ, and then help them grow in the faith through prayer meetings, Bible study, and revival services. The church was also concerned about mission, not in its own community but overseas. Unfortunately, the congregation not only had little concern for its immediate community, it actually caused divisions in the community. It separated longtime friends and even family members from each other. It caused alienation in some of the groups working for social betterment. Harm was done in the name of the "pure faith." The congregation created an unhealthy spirit in the community. It was in that sense an anticreative force.

Other congregations have erred on the other side, however. One particular church in a large Midwestern city was so concerned about issues of community justice that it did not concern itself with the well-being of its members. Eventually, without nurture, they simply "burned out," drifted away from the congregation, letting the church fold. This congregation left the lives of its members in disorder—broken people. It was anticreative for them, even though it had some victories earlier in terms of creative community change.

Organizations can and should make it possible for people to become more fully human because of creative interaction. Yet, frequently, organizations become a means of control by oppressing their own constituents and, secondly, by imposing the will of the group on the lives of others. When an organization functions negatively to control both its constituents and other people, both groups are oppressed. It puts the controller and the controllee in an adversary position which limits the creative possibilities of both. Thus organizations, at whatever level, can become means of oppression. This happened in both congregations described above in the name of either piety or social justice.

Traditional role definition, formalized relationships, and assumptions about reality are all challenged if one is to deal with issues creatively. To do this would cause significant social upheaval, a price that many people are unwilling to pay. This means that organizations, at whatever sphere or level, can and do function to lessen our humanity. This is group sin. It oppresses both the dominant and the minority in that organizational milieu.

There are many responses in organizational life to group sin, anticreativity, or oppression. When an organization fails to meet the needs of a large minority of persons, it also hurts the organization's controlling majority—unless they are willing to deal with that minority in a creative fashion. The minority often possess liberating creativity that can free the majority. If the majority deal with the minority creatively, both can benefit.

However, the tendency is to try to protect the past. When this is done, the move toward preservation of the status quo effectively blocks the organization from creative participation in ongoing history. Relatively, affirming the status quo causes the organization to get out of touch with ongoing needs and it increasingly becomes a useless or even oppressive organization. Some in the organization wish to protect past values. These are the conservatives. Others in the organization wish to protect past organizational styles, functioning as reactionaries. A small minority in a dominant organization may become very disenchanted with the inability of the organization to deal with the creative minority and they become the revolutionaries. However, their revolutionary nature usually means that they end up excluded from the dominant decision-making role in that organization. Still others in the organization, even though affirming the past, may try to maintain some balance between past values and the past organizational system. These are the persons who try to rehabilitate or revise the organization in the light of present circumstances, but still affirm the past values and styles of doing business.

When an organization enters into a stage of life where it affirms the status quo, frustration among those within the organization as well as among those who are excluded from the organization is usually very high. There are typically three responses that participants make to this stage in the anticreative activity of organizational life. The first of these is apathy. Apathy is that normal human response to the milieu which is either too complex or too painful to deal with. It immobilizes, it saps energy, and it leads to attempts at "business as usual." The second response is a negative but conscious response. This response usually is typified by an attempt to return to a previous state of "bliss." In today's church, for example, this response is typically an attempt to return to the "good old days" of the 1950s when the church was an elitist powerful organization. Such a response leads to attempts at consolidation of current resources around past values. In some ways this response is a "head in the sand" response, because it ignores the realities of the current situation and tries to interpret the current situation in the light of a once-remembered past glory.

The third response in a status quo organization is rage. It is a response that can be made by those within the organization who are extremely frustrated and oppressed by it as well as by the creative minority who are excluded from the dominant organization. Rage is that growing emotion emerging from frustration which bursts forth in some form of radical action. The radical action may be either creative or destructive, but it has as its goal the destruction of the status quo. In its worst form, it produces a kind of nihilism destroying for destruction's sake. In its best form, it becomes a force that rebuilds some new, creative, and less oppressive styles of organizational life—both for those within and for those outside the organization.

These three responses that emerge from frustration with the status quo organization can be disintegrative and anticreative. However, there is a fourth possible creative response that may emerge from involvement in an oppressing organization. The Christian gospel indicates that it should be the normative response for those consciously participating as co-creators and as persons of faith and hope. This is the creative response. What is creativity? Creativity is the product of cooperation among those who share the frustration that causes them ultimately to transcend the current malaise. Creativity is not the normal result of frustration. It must be struggled for, and out of the struggle comes the kind of positive interaction that can release the oppression experienced by both the oppressor and the oppressed. Creativity builds a whole new synthesis of reality. It creates new mythic foundations, values, based on that understanding of reality. It produces the kinds of actions that release energy rather than control energy. It is the gift of God for those who will join in the struggle against the preservation of the status quo in the quest for wholeness.

IN AND BEYOND TIME

The conclusion to this chapter's opening story about an urban New England church becomes a paradigm. The predominant mood of the congregation's members was apathy. Most, initially, were overwhelmed by the malaise. Yet a few among them were responsive to probes to help them redefine their historical circumstances and their ministry in that situation. For a whole year, they tried to think new thoughts, dream new dreams, and build trusting relationships with three other congregations in similar circumstances traditionally competitors. One of those other churches was in an urban renewal area and had to sell its building. Another had so few members it could not economically survive. The third was in a similar situation. Together these congregations began a cooperative youth program for the dozen or so young people they had among them. Then they were able to share in a community ministry in one of the four church buildings. They pooled resources and hired a deaconess to minister to the elderly. Next, they worshiped and studied together. Finally, they began to dream of a new kind of mission in the heart of the city—a new reason for being. To the surprise of all, it was unexpectedly proposed by the parish council established at the end of the first year that these congregations merge into one fellowship and build a new kind of congregation, building, and ministry for the city rather than for themselves. As they were helped to assess the dynamics at work in their life, and as they understood the gospel, the world, and themselves in progressive rather than status quo terms, the gift of creativity broke through and they transcended their own traditions. The result of the process was greater creativity than any one of the preceding parties had by itself.

This experience leads one to reflect on a final concern of this chapter. It has to do with an understanding of an organization's corporate nature. Most church persons, for example, are person-oriented. The people in the churches just mentioned really assumed that a congregation or an organization was merely the sum of the people who are participants. This assumption is like saying the body is merely the sum of the heart, liver, brain, eyes, ears, etc. The human body is more than the sum of these parts. It transcends them to include the spirit, creativity, and being —that which differentiates one person from another, although both have the similar parts. But how does any organization in general and these congregations in particular transcend the sum of their parts? Why did they develop a life of their own greater than the sum of their constituents' segments?

An organization has life which transcends the lives of those who currently participate in several ways. First, these congregations, as with any organization, became a means by which people were able to participate in the broader purposes of history—in this case, a very dramatically changed city. Most people are not conscious of this possibility and tend to see the purposes of their organizations in a much more limited sense. They see them as simply serving their own day-to-day social, religious, economic, political, and educational needs. Secondly, a congregation or an organization transcends the lives of individual participants in history, growing, flourishing, and then usually declining. This idea will be explored later.

An organization's life transcends the individual participants in still another way. It co-opts them into the dreams and aspirations of those who have gone before. Members of each of the four congregations knew the myths of how effective their churches had once been. Because of the nurturing functions of an organization, people are caused to buy into assumptions and dreams that they did not create, but that, rather, were created by their forebears. The success of the forebears provides hope.

Finally, a church, like any other organization, has a life of its own in the sense that it is one small part of a total pattern of culture and civilization which is more influential in the lives of individuals than most would perceive. Even if organizational participants make a conscious decision to dissolve an organization because of a nihilistic or anti-institutional bias, the odds are great that consequently they will create some new organizational forms instead. Even if the new organizational forms differ in style, the forms would still be considered a part of an overall directional pattern. They simply have adapted into the overall cultural myth, in a new way.

Chapter IV

CHANGE

THE CONCEPT OF CHANGE has to do with the fundamental concept of the nature of God. God is procreator,
or the purposeful creator. We have suggested that the
creation is a manifestation of God's creativity, that God is
the organizing principle which makes it possible for the
primordial stuff—the primordial chaos—to increasingly
develop interrelationships of wholeness. Organizations,
and organizational relationships, are intricately related in
both positive and negative ways to the process of change.
They are a means by which humankind participates in, or
impedes, the process of creation. Therefore, how do organizations either enhance or negate the creative change
process?

Three groups had moved into South County, Indiana, by
the middle of the nineteenth century: German Catholics,
German Lutherans, and a group comprised of a few other
German Protestants and a great number of Appalachian
whites. Through the end of the nineteenth century these
three groups had built a rather prosperous agrarian society. The religious differences, however, kept the groups
separate even though they lived in neighboring communities. By the early 1900s, religion became the means of

maintaining separation among the three segments of the population. Since the three were evenly balanced, they thought one another standoffish—and refused to change the status gap. The static nature of this county made it less and less viable economically and socially. From 1920 on to the 1960s the county showed a significant decline in population. The poverty level in the county showed signs of increase; the educational achievement of the residents of the county fell behind the state as a whole. In short, the county was becoming an increasingly more difficult place in which to live because societal life had stopped growing there.

In the mid-1960s right after the excitement of Vatican II, the churches in the county decided that something needed to be done for both religious and social renewal. For seven years the leaders of the churches worked together to build communication among the three segments of the population. A small nucleus of religious leaders in the county rethought what it meant to be a Christian in that milieu. These actions, in turn, began to stimulate the people in the county to work creatively. The communication encouraged interaction that heretofore had not been occurring. And the rethinking process, based upon serious Bible study by a core of leaders, gave new ideas that could energize the community. In the fifth, sixth, and seventh years the community began to renew its educational institutions, began to become innovative in providing new economic opportunities for the area, and ultimately began to reshape the religious institutions in the county. These forces in interaction meant that by the end of seven years, the county had begun to develop economically, and it had begun to show an increase in population. And in general, the quality of life had begun to improve also.

SOME THEOLOGICAL OBSERVATIONS
ABOUT ORGANIZATIONAL CHANGE

The South County experience and many others raise the questions, What is change? and Why is there change—in our culture, in our society, in a congregation, and in our organizations? The question, What is change? is a sociological question, and the question, Why is there change? is a philosophical and theological question. Many people have dealt with the questions about change by ignoring them. Others have dealt with change by actively supporting the status quo. And still others have acted as agents of change in their organizations, neighborhoods, and communities. Some have even reflected on why change occurs. These normal human reactions relate, in part, to the psychic makeup of the persons, but they are also related to the organizational and cultural style of the society.

As suggested earlier, an understanding of creation as developing implies that change is to be expected. Even when South County was actively affirming the status quo, negative change was occurring. The attempts at renewal were attempts toward positive change. Change for change's sake is not necessarily good, but directional change toward fulfillment and wholeness is the norm of creation. For the Christian, purposeful change is to be expected and encouraged. To be a participant with the Creator in ongoing creation requires participation in those changes which work toward wholeness and fulfillment.

Some reactions to change may be destructive. For example, Adolf Hitler was instrumental in creating significant change in the world. To a large extent, he responded to growing cultural diversity by trying to affirm the primacy of the northern European white Christian. By any measure of justice, self-determination, and universal wholeness, the system that he devised was anticreative, selfish, self-serving, and demonic. He tried to exclude whole segments of the world's population from participation in their own destiny, and subjugated the rights of the masses to the needs of the few, creating new depths of oppression. Consequently, at that point in the world's history, the creative action was to oppose these demonic forces so that all persons could be free of Hitler and participate in their own destiny.

Constructive change means not standing still. White settlers first came to South County to create a new life for themselves away from the oppression they had experienced in the old country. But as that generation's creativity ran its course, the resulting patterns became oppressive to the next generation. Likewise, the United States and its allies responded in a creative fashion to the challenges that Hitler provided. But in so doing, they became stultifying in the 1950s and 1960s, particularly in terms of the aspirations of emerging peoples—those in Africa, the Middle East, Southeast Asia, the Caribbean, and South America. The result was that the United States now often finds itself in the strange position of affirming the dictators and the colonial powers who represent the status quo and who are denying the just aspirations of the oppressed of this generation. Creative change is a struggle toward wholeness and against the tendency toward equilibrium or the status quo.

DYNAMICS WITHIN AN ORGANIZATION

At their best, organizations in general and congregations in particular produce the means by which human beings can participate in the ongoing purposes of creation. They can do this in several ways. The first is through nurture. The nurturing function relates to the ways in which participants intensify relationships with each other and their purpose in the congregation or an organization. This function provides the opportunity for people to interact around their mutual concerns, to develop their common perceptions of reality, to understand the dimensions of their concerns, and to devise ways whereby they can participate in the broader dimensions of society around their central concern. Further, nurturing provides an opportunity to build group cohesiveness. To a large extent, this is what was happening in South County when the leaders interacted for the first three years in Bible study. The group gave them an opportunity to discover who they were together, to discover their common values and perspectives, and to create the common values that gave them cohesiveness as a group.

The nurturing function at its worst can become narcissistic. At its best, it can become the vehicle that provides opportunities for creative participation in the ongoing dimensions of history. Early church history offers an example. Through Paul, the embryonic churches were able to define how they were different from Jewish and Hellenistic religion and culture. In so doing, they were able to build community solidarity in terms of an underlying rationale or set of values which motivated them to perceive the reality of the situation differently from those around them. They were able to differentiate themselves from their peers and reinforce this identity.

The nurturing function of differentiation within an organization or a congregation can become self-defeating, however, unless there is also provision for a second major function to take place creatively. That is the outreach or task function. This function provides a way by which the members can focus their energies so that what they have experienced in the congregation can be shared with others. In other words, an organization also functions to pro-

vide means by which the organization's participants may
influence the larger community. This fact became very
evident in South County when from the nurturing Bible
study group a different mission developed. A retired mail-
man who had been a part of the group became quite
concerned about the poverty of the area. One day he went
with a Catholic priest from the group to the state capital
to encourage state officials to provide food stamps in the
county when the county commissioners refused to do so.
As a result of that trip, and of several other actions taken
in the county, the welfare system there was modified significantly.

This experience and numerous others indicate that
there are two dimensions to outreach. First, it enables
people in a group to focus their energy and resources so
that they can make their presence felt in the broader
community. Second, it enables the group to develop symbols that can communicate their perspectives with the
experiences and thought categories of the dominant culture. Therefore, part of the outreach function is the per-
petual task of translating the organization's self-under-
standing—i.e., their reason for being—into symbols that
can in turn relate to the understandings and needs of the
larger culture. For example, from a sociological perspective the Christian church would have been far different
without the skills and abilities of the apostle Paul to help
differentiate Christianity from its surroundings. It is
equally true, however, that the church would not have so
prospered in the first century had it not developed skill in
relating Christian thought categories to the Hellenistic
philosophical foundations of the Greco-Roman culture.
Paul did this by giving Christian experience symbolic
meanings which the Greeks and the Romans could relate
to their cultural experience. At the same time that Paul
was developing these symbols which could be understood
by Greeks or Romans, he was also providing the means for

the small band of Christians to multiply and make an impact upon that culture.

Outreach with nurturing enabled the churches in South County to become wholistic organizations with a self-reinforcing identity that could interact with the dominant culture. Nurture and outreach are in tension, however. Nurture builds group intensity, and conditions people to differentiate themselves from the broader community. It builds links with the past as well as solidarity in the present. In a sense, it is like pouring water into a jar—but if you only pour water in, and provide no opportunity for any escape, it soon becomes stagnant. This may happen in a congregation or any organization. Only if provision is made for the internal resources resulting from the nurturing process to be shared with the outside community does the group gain dynamic life. The outreach function provides this opportunity. On the other hand, if the group exists only for outreach, it will soon find itself cut off from its internal resources and its reason for being—cut off from what itself motivates outreach. The group becomes "cut-stem flowers," with a life that temporarily flourishes but is unable to continue without roots. Thus it is through keeping these two functions in balanced interaction that a congregation or an organization lives.

These are the general ways, then, that an organization mobilizes itself for meaningful participation in the larger human community. There are, however, demands put upon an organization by society. Society expects any congregation or organization to play out two broader functions. The first expectation is for the organization to help conserve those values which previous experience has proven are vital to society. This is to say that unless an organization helps its societal matrix to conserve some of society's basic values as a gift back to that society, the organization will be perceived as a parasite or threat to the host society. This need not be affirmation of the status quo.

Rather, it might be reinterpretation which helps the dominant society to see how certain values which historically gave meaning to that society can be reinterpreted to give meaning to the emerging situation. Two examples might be helpful. In South County, religion was functioning exclusively to conserve the past and to impede the present, sapping creative possibilities. Another example might have to do with the Western culture itself. As the industrial revolution developed, the historic values of individual human worth, freedom, and rights clashed with productivity, so that by the 1850s society was very oppressive to workers. It was within this context, in the late nineteenth century, that the social gospel arose. It was able to build patterns of interaction between the historic values and the needs of industrial society which renewed the dignity of the individual.

When conserving past values becomes an end in itself, it begins to affirm the status quo. It is at this point that the second societal expectation of congregations and organizations must be played out—i.e., being the conscience or prophet. Organizations must help the larger society to see those points of weakness and self-indulgence where creativity is being impeded. The social gospel movement of the late nineteenth century and the early twentieth century was able to perform that creative function. The small Bible study group in South County provided a similar function. Both developed the criticism that ultimately helped the society in the county to clarify and build new basic values which were needed for creativity.

The prophetic function is never an easy one, and yet subconsciously the society expects a congregation or an organization to serve this function. This was illustrated some years ago. During the height of the labor unrest between the miners and the strip mine owners in the Southeast, a church worker (with blue jeans, beard, and long hair) stopped there for gasoline. He did not notice that the car on the other side of the gas pump belonged to a deputy sheriff. The church worker casually asked the attendant what was new that morning with the strike. The deputy sheriff heard that question and spotted his attire and long hair. He jumped out of his car, came over to the church worker, and said, "I suppose you are one of those labor organizers and rabblerousers." The worker was shocked and a little overwhelmed but finally stammered: "No, no. I am on the staff of the Council of Churches." Thereupon the deputy sheriff said: "That's even worse! The church shouldn't be involved in these kinds of problems." This incident illustrates quite vividly the sheriff's assumption that the church would be involved prophetically in that labor conflict. Actually, the church was not; the church worker was in that area organizing people to develop low-cost housing for the rural elderly poor. Nonetheless, even critical people expect churches, as well as other organizations, to be their conscience—speaking out on social issues, pushing for creative change. Amazingly, people even support the church financially knowing it will challenge common anticreative practices they enjoy.

If the organization only assists the dominant society in conserving values, it soon becomes captive of the dominant society. In a religious institution, this would mean that the religious group would be perpetuating a civic religion, or the mind-set that leads people to say, "My country, right or wrong, but my country." On the other hand, if the organization exists only to engage in the conscious prophetic functions, soon the organization has so little credibility in the dominant society that it is not listened to. Therefore these conserving and prophetic functions must be kept in balance if an organization is to provide a viable model to the larger community. Without the freshness and creativity resulting from this balance, the church becomes anticreative and fails to move forward, because it is no longer serving the best interests of its constituents, nor is it dynamically interacting with its environment.

Hence, in proper proportions outreach and nurture, as well as the conservation of values and the prophetic conscience, determine organization vitality. Creativity comes from the balanced tension among these four functions.

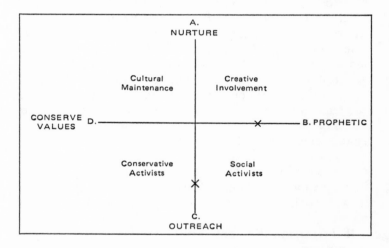

Ideally, a balanced organization would participate in all four directions and thus would function near the intersection of the diagram. In fact, many have varied characteristics. For example, organizations oriented to social change function well in prophetic roles and outreach but may have difficulty perpetuating themselves because they lack nurturing to members and the credibility of conserving values. They may be perceived as being in opposition to dominant society.

Some conservative religious activists and some groups such as the John Birch Society are examples of organizations strong on outreach and maintaining traditional values.

Organizations such as the Scouts, civic clubs, and sororities often are conserving societal values with the purpose primarily of nurturing their constituency. On the other hand, organizations strong on nurture and prophetic confrontation would include progressive enterprises that build a constituency and nurture them to work at the growing edge of society. The World Future Society, a professional association of some sixteen thousand members, is a good illustration. It is a scholarly group that continually looks to the emerging needs of society through study, dialogue, and gentle pressure on the status quo.

Organizations with broad purposes, like the church, the government, the schools, and industries, must be active in varying degrees in all four quadrants, while special purpose organizations may concentrate in only one or two quadrants. Others must then complement them by functioning in the other quadrants. For example, the Scouts, civic groups, YMCA and YWCA, and fraternal and sorority organizations are voluntary organizations to serve the needs of the community. Within society in a given area, they need to develop activity in each of the four quadrants so that volunteer participation in the community can remain healthy. It may mean that if a specific club is functioning in quadrant AB (nurture-prophetic), the YMCA and sororities functioning in quadrant BC (prophetic-outreach), fraternities in the quadrant CD (outreach-conserving), and the Scouts in quadrant DA (conserving-nurture), they complement each other to the benefit of their community. On the other hand, if all function in a single quadrant, the effect would be disadvantageous to the community. In this case the voluntary system would not be carrying its responsibility and the community would suffer. Health in any congregation or community organization or community is manifested by dynamic balance of the forces represented by the four poles. Stagnation often results when a congregation or an organization is acting in only one quadrant.

ORGANIZATIONAL CHANGE
IN THE CULTURAL CONTEXT

Interaction among the four functions affects the congregational and organizational life. Equally important for organizational life, however, is the interaction between the organization and its cultural milieu. As they interact, change occurs in the organization as well as in the culture. Numerous theories have been developed on the nature of social change. The discipline of sociology arose as a means of exploring the changes that take place within the society and, to some extent, between societies. Much of the philosophy of history has evolved from the need of humankind to explain the rise and fall of civilizations and the conflict that results from changes which developed because of the interaction among civilizations. Some theories of social change are incremental—i.e., change is seen as evolutionary, slow-moving, and directional. Other theorists have developed sophisticated theories about equilibrium, saying that the human organization, at whatever level, is always seeking an equilibrium. According to this view, when internal or external forces cause the organization to be in disequilibrium, the organization always strives to regain its equilibrium. Still other theorists, who might be called "systems theorists," have undertaken to understand the interaction among a very complex mix of factors or groups as being the principal means through which change can be explained. Systems theory draws on both incremental and equilibrium theories but uses the concept of power. It emphasizes the power that one part of the system can exert on another part in terms of kind and in terms of scale. In many ways, the "systems" understanding of social change is the most adequate because it deals with both complexity and wholeness. For example, it can explain the actions of congregations, presbyteries, synods, and general church agencies, which are connected and influence each other, but which also contribute to the church as a whole and the society generally. All social characteristics derive from such processes and organizational patterns and contribute to one all-inclusive process of cosmic evolution. In this wholistic "systems" view, which is ultimately a dynamic view of social organizational change, there are qualities which we call life, spirituality, consciousness, self-consciousness, reason, and these provide the energy for the system. This energy allows freedom, free will, power, and human autonomy to play a role in the direction in which the system moves. The result is not predetermined. In a theological sense, if people are faithful, faith can lead to creation's fulfillment; but if forces prevail that are counter to creation, destruction might result. These conflicting forces, which are not well understood scientifically, mean that nonpredictable change can occur because the interaction among the parts can develop a kind of life of its own. Much change is unpredictable, therefore. But always the dynamics within an organization and other parts of the social system have a mutual effect upon each other. This is to say that society is a symbiotic or mutually beneficial relationship of organizations embodying a variety of skills and kinds. For example, in the Bible study in South County the forces were at work which helped people grow in their understanding of their role in that society. As they began to mature in their spiritual understanding, "spirit" caused several other things to happen that ultimately influenced the whole countywide socioeconomic system as well as the religious ecclesiastical structure. The unpredictability of such forces as spirituality, however, means that social engineering is nearly an impossibility. It also means that planned social change will never have the results that are planned, because the multiple number of variables interacting to influence any given plan of change is always greater than the planner's ability to comprehend.

Simplistic views of change rarely work; rather, they usually produce more adverse circumstances than the problems which they were designed to solve. There are a number of reasons, but among them is that many of the assumptions and technologies of current planners are obsolete and meaningless. They do not take into consideration their dated philosophical assumptions of the mind, the spirit, the flesh, matter, energy, free will, humankind, science, religion, man, and society. For example, the assumption that urban blight is bad is based upon an even earlier assumption that humankind must and probably will continue to live in cities. Therefore, during the 1960s, massive programs were developed to demolish existing substandard housing patterns and put in their place massive apartment complexes, many of which were organized around a garden apartment concept. Eventually, some of these early urban renewal projects had to be torn down. The reasons revolved largely around the fact that the community planners were unable to deal with the relationships between physical milieu and human interaction. In Boston, for example, an old Italian area had a pattern of social control based on a physical arrangement that had all the children playing in the streets while the elderly sat at the windows or on the front stoops and watched the children. The elderly took responsibility for all the children and promptly scolded them if they got out of hand. When garden apartments replaced the previous slum dwellings, the eyes of the older adults were turned inward toward the garden. The children continued to play in the parking lots that surrounded the outside of the buildings and the service areas that gave access to the apartments from the back. Without the subtle control exercised by the elders in an informal situation, the parking lots and service areas became areas of vandalism, theft, and assault.

Change, then, even on the most realistic set of assumptions cannot be specifically predicted. Yet general trends are often discernible. One can say that social change is influenced by a number of factors. Among them are: (a) the social context—where the group finds itself in the overall social environment; (b) allocated time—involving the values of the group; (c) technology—useful patterns of interaction between human resources and material resources; (d) the physical environment, including raw materials, geography, and climate; and (e) finally, the people themselves, the number of persons, their psychic outlook, the complexity of the organizations they develop, and their general ability to respond to circumstances. Despite the interplay of factors, the individual person of faith has the freedom and responsibility to participate in causes that work toward justice and wholeness.

ORGANIZATIONS AND NEEDS

Sometime ago, Abraham Maslow theorized that a person has a hierarchy of needs. Essentially, the thesis is that people meet first their most fundamental needs—for food, for warmth and clothing, and for shelter. After these needs are taken care of, people try to meet their secondary needs for personal fulfillment. These secondary needs include the need for knowledge, which gives rise to education; the need for beauty, which gives rise to the arts; and the need for spiritual fulfillment, which gives rise to religion. Maslow's observations also contribute to an understanding of relationships among organizations, communities, societies, cultures, and civilizations. For example, when a community has successfully met its primary needs —food, clothing, and shelter—the purposes of the suborganizations within that broader community system also have to be modified if they are to remain viable as organizations. Fundamental needs are met and will continue to be met because the system is working well for the majority. Therefore, the second level of needs becomes the dominant concern of that community. If the organizations in that community are unwilling or unable to help that community meet the second level of needs, their usefulness to the total community will decline. The same argument can be made in terms of the larger societal context as well as the context of culture and civilization.

These differences in the ability to meet fundamental needs in different levels of organization and in different civilizations can be the cause of significant strife. Nowhere is this more evident than in the strife between the first and second and third worlds. The first and second worlds have to a large extent met their basic needs for the majority of their constituents—food, clothing, and shelter are no longer a problem. Therefore, their attention turns to more remote concerns which relate to the need for knowledge, the need for spiritual fulfillment, and the need for cultural fulfillment through the arts. Therefore, the first and second worlds are allocating a greater proportion of their resources in these directions with little apparent concern for the fact that the third world is still struggling to meet the most fundamental human needs. If the first and second worlds are not responsive to the needs of the third world, the third world is not being allowed to play the role of a critical, creative minority. This neglect may result in revolution, and the third world may become an invading crowd that will destroy the sophistication of the first and second worlds. This destruction would come because third world people have not been allowed to participate in the affluent first and second worlds, even to have their most basic needs met. In frustration, the only responses open to the third world are the ones described above—apathy, creativity, or nihilism. Because apathy cannot last forever and because their creativity is rejected by the first and second worlds' civilizations, nihilism may become the only alternative open to them. These conflicts, played out on whatever scale, may exert tremendous force upon any organization in any of the systems. Therefore, even though an organization is adequately providing for the needs for which it was originated, it may find itself in deep difficulty, because it has not consciously responded to the needs of the larger context. Only as organizations are renewed and begin to transcend historic patterns can they participate in renewal of the entire, perhaps global, community.

Chapter V

LIFE CYCLES

THE LIFE of an organization is affected by three factors: the tendency of creation to change in the direction of wholeness; the way an organization works internally; and the way an organization interacts with the rest of society. There is, however, a fourth factor which plays an important role in organizational life. It is the life cycle of an organization. Organizations, like people, go through a life cycle. The span of that life cycle varies significantly in terms of the complexity and functions of the organization in the broader context of society. For example, some voluntary organizations have a very brief life cycle compared to the life cycles of nations, societies, or whole cultures. Nonetheless, understanding the life cycle of an organization helps us to understand change within organizations as it relates to the broader changes in the overall dominant culture.

Most of us have had experience with congregations or organizations that are at different points in their life. The congregation in the county seat town referred to in the first chapter was effectively serving its community. The New England urban congregation was in serious decline. Some churches are completely static—dead, going through the motions of life. New organizations are also being created, but beginning organizations differ significantly from most effective organizations as well as from declining or dying ones.

Where an organization is in terms of its own internal life cycle determines to a large measure the effectiveness of its interaction with its broader social environment. For example, the life cycle of a congregation or an organization might be looked at in terms of the challenges or obstacles it must overcome. When an organization is young it frequently faces an obstacle related to the contending leaders' "jockeying" for position. If it resolves this and grows, its work often proliferates and results in a variety of task, action, or functional groups with each tending to become autonomous and "doing its own thing." Unless these parts develop complementary goals that help the whole congregation or organization to move in a common direction, the centrifugal force will cause the congregation to split, divide, or otherwise come "unglued." This potential is often solved administratively by exerting more controls over the parts. In a church this is usually a pastor or key leader stepping in and controlling, by force of personality, all the parts. In other kinds of organization it is often done with new rules and more "red tape." Either way, the organization is taken away from the people and an obstacle of credibility results. This can be overcome by moving to a more shared leadership and organizational style. If an organization is unable to move through this obstacle course successfully, it will die. The way an organization deals with these obstacles affects not only its creativity but its usefulness to the broader community.

Although this perspective on a congregation's or an organization's potential obstacles gives some clues to the internal dynamics of organizational life, the dynamics are, in fact, much more complex than this obstacle analysis indicates. It is fitting to ponder these dynamics in more detail, because they are directly related to the role and function of organizations in God's creation and the role and function of congregations in their community.

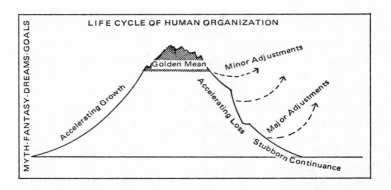

DYNAMICS OF ORGANIZATIONAL GROWTH

In broad sweeps, the phases in the growth process are as follows: First, commonly perceived needs bring persons together for the purpose of seeing whether or not they can meet those needs. Secondly, as they begin to meet their own needs, they also begin to demonstrate to the larger community that they are a viable organization. The community begins to gain confidence in them and more persons join the organization. Finally, the organization attains a sustained plateau or "golden mean" in its life. Briefly put, this describes the internal dynamics which cause and guide the process whether it be a congregation or any other organization. But what are the detailed dynamics in the organization's life that make it grow?

Psychological Milieu

The first general dynamic has to do with the psychological milieu. The growth of an organization is directly related to the psychological milieu of the community. The psychological milieu has to do with felt needs that interact to make it possible for an organization to be needed and to grow. These felt needs give rise to myths, beliefs, attitudes, and mores by which the action of the organization is directed and sanctioned. The psychological milieu provides the common perceptions of reality held by the members of the group around which they organize their lives. These perceptions are not necessarily rational but they do deal with fundamental perceptions of reality. They are the product of the interaction between the individuals who share a need and their cultural milieu.

Myths, which are basic motivating understandings about reality on which we act, in turn give rise to beliefs and attitudes. Beliefs are rational or rationalized manifestations of myths. Beliefs emerge out of the interaction between the myth and the cultural milieu. Beliefs are statements by which individuals order their lives. They have a degree of inflexibility and they tend to be localized. On the other hand, attitudes are the product of the interaction between beliefs and the historical world in which the participants of the organization live. Attitudes always have a degree of pragmatism involved in them, even though they have roots in beliefs and in the myths by which the persons order their lives. Attitudes are more existential in the sense that they change from day to day as the cultural milieu and the basic mythic and belief structure of the person interact.

The third force in the psychological dimensions of organizational dynamics includes mores. Mores are the patterns of behavior expected from the participants in the

organizations. They rise out of the prevailing myths, beliefs, and attitudes within the organizations. Mores in-
volve patterned channeling of the compromises that the
participants in the organization make on a day-to-day
basis so that they can get along with each other. They are
patterns of action which are generally held by the constituents of that organization to be acceptable. If a person breaks the pattern of mores, sanctions are frequently
placed against him or her by the rest of the organization.
These force compliance. If there is not compliance, the
result is usually banishment or exclusion from the organization.

Similar patterns develop in congregations. Many congregations develop strong myths, beliefs, and attitudes
about what constitutes Christian behavior. These range
from such innocuous demands as no smoking, drinking,
dancing, or going to movies to much more serious demands about what one can believe, how one should relate
to other community organizations and to the "unbeliev-
ers" in one's family or the community, and with whom one
should do business. Nonconformity may result in cold-
shoulder practices that effectively, but informally, banish
persons from the congregation. They often just do not
attend anymore. The congregation may then pray for the
"back-slider" not realizing that they caused the predicament or, in some cases, that their pressure had deeply
harmed the person. The psychodynamics within an organization can be severe. They can also be constructive in
other situations.

Roles of Members

The second general dynamic has to do with the roles
that participants play in the organization or the congregation. To a large extent, the way these roles are played by
the constituents and the way they interact determines the

growth of the organization. These roles may be competitive or they may be complementary, but the dominant roles played in the organization as it is growing are significantly different from the roles played in an organization in decline. If the organization is to grow, a symbiotic relationship develops among these roles to produce a kind of creativity in that organization which makes it viable in the broader society. What are these roles?

The feeling role is first. This role in the organizational growth process is played by those who are able to sense the needs of a group. The organization begins to mature when persons who are engaged in the feeling role tend to be past-oriented. That is, they help the group relate what is presently occurring to that which has brought warmth, security, and success to the organization in its previous experiences. The person who plays the feeling role frequently is good at verbalizing the deepest feelings of a group so that the rest of the group can relate to them as well.

The second role is the intuitive role. The intuitive role is played by those who are good with hunches and who do the right thing without quite knowing why. These persons tend to be future-oriented and their intuitive nature tends to relate the current situation to that which the organization must do in the future, if it is to be successful. Intuitive persons are not usually good at verbalizing or analyzing the present. Rather, they are on the growing edge, sensing what must be done for a creative future.

A third role that seems to predominate in the growing organization is the practical role. The persons who play this role are those who continually ask: Will it work? Is it practical? These persons are present-oriented. They help the group keep its feet on the ground.

The last role that is played by members of a growing organization might be called the rational role. The persons who play this role continually help the group keep in touch with its myth—its values and reason for being. They are continually involved in remythologizing the reason for the organization's being. Their contribution to the ongoing life of the organization lies in their ability to continually tell the story that gave rise to the organization's being in the light of the present circumstances and their future hopes. These are the persons who do the ongoing planning for the group. They are engaged in the past, present, and future, and they combine the orientations of the feeling role, the intuitive role, and the practical role to forge the future of that organization. In a growing congregation or organization, the intuitive and rational roles must have ascendancy over the feeling and practical roles, but all must be present.

Translation of Myth to Reality

Beyond the psychological milieu and the roles that the constituents play, there is still a third major dynamic that makes an organization or a congregation grow. This is the process by which the organization translates myth into reality. One of the basic concepts of sociology is self-fulfilling prophecy, that is, people tend to cause to happen that which they think is going to happen. Myth reflects that which people believe to be reality. A growing organization must successfully translate its myth about reality into fantasy. Fantasy transcends reality. But fantasy also provides the opportunity for wild thoughts—thoughts that make imaginings about utopia possible. The constituency of an organization must be able to fantasize together. "What would it be like if our organization had a ministry to every individual on every continent in the world?" is a fantasy shared by members of one Christian missionary organization. But fantasies must give way to the next stage of mobilizing energy—dreaming. Out of the fantasy phase an organization develops some dreams that begin to interweave fantasy with reality. These dreams are inevitably future-oriented and they are stimulated by the intuitive, rational, feeling, and practical roles that constituents of that organization are playing. When an organization reaches this stage, the intuitive and rational roles must have ascendancy over the feeling and practical roles if there is to be accelerating growth. If one is too past-oriented and/or too practical, one cannot dream a dream that is creative enough to make the organization grow.

The mind-stretching experiences of fantasizing and dreaming must then be translated into action. The common mode for doing this is to build goals from the best of the fantasy and dream sequences. Goals help to actualize dreams. Goals are statements about conditions which the organization wishes to see in the future and yet which are realistic enough that the constituents of the organization are willing to invest their time and energy to cause these goals to be realized. Thus, goals become the commonly accepted agendas for the action of the organization. The goal that is enough future-oriented and shared by the group usually makes it possible for that organization to show a pattern of accelerating growth. This is particularly apparent if the organization's goals make it possible for its nucleus group to meet some of the needs of the community at large.

Many things begin to happen to the organizational nucleus when it starts to grow. As the psychological milieu, the role of constituents, the mythic foundations, and the psychological mobilization of the constituents take place, an organizational system begins to emerge. That which began with a great intensity of feeling by a few begins to include more persons who originally were less committed.

Gradually as the organization develops and grows, that intensive feeling must be revised in such ways that more and more people can identify with the underlying myth. This development is the movement from the fantasy stage to the dream stage to the goal stage. By the time the organization is showing maximum growth, the organization tends to be a very open system that is accepting new ideas and relationships with people who are not of the same background. The organization has a perspective and a point of view, but it is open for interaction with anyone who is willing to participate in that point of view. Consequently, its ability to serve a broader community is at its optimum. Concern about formal constitutions and bylaws is slight. Minimal effort is needed to keep the organization together. There is flexibility, purpose, and openness in this kind of organization.

But as the organization moves toward the plateau of the growth stage, the system begins to close. The organizational system now follows the style in which it is comfortable. It has a patterned way of doing things. There are formalized patterns of behavior and actions that are expected. Creativity begins to give way to bureaucratization, professional staff, and reduced psychic involvement on the part of the people. Bureaucratization has to do with a clearly defined hierarchy of jobs and tasks in an organization, and communication is from top to bottom, not vice versa. The organization is very formal. People come, they participate in a *pro forma* fashion, but they do not really give of themselves to the organization, they do only what is expected and paid for. The organization, as a result, gives of itself to the broader community only in prescribed fashions. This period in the organization's life may go on for a great length of time or it may move immediately into a phase of decline in organizational viability.

DYNAMICS OF ORGANIZATIONAL DECLINE

What are the dynamics that cause an organization or a congregation to move from its initial creativity to an anti-creative, declining, and crystallizing organization? Just as part of the reason for an organization's growth lies in its organizational dynamics, so part of the reason for its decline lies in its internal dynamics. As an organization becomes closed from interaction with society, choosing to serve the few rather than the many, the problems it faces will tend to multiply more rapidly than they can be resolved. In fact, some say that the more skilled the leadership of an organization is in classical organizational problem-solving, at this point in its life cycle, the more likely it is that the organization will be in deep organizational trouble. As an organization becomes more and more closed from interaction with its constituency and its environment, a minority of persons realize that the organization is getting out of touch with reality. They begin to put pressure on the organization for creative changes. When these changes do not occur, the people become disenchanted or deviant. The organization usually responds to deviation in two ways. First, it will develop new procedural rules to control the organization. These procedural rules usually result in a development of secondary rewards for conformity to the norms established during the time of organizational growth. When this happens, the life dynamics become a chronicle of anticreativity or of the development of group sin.

An illustration familiar to church people involved a church school. The church school had been successful in attracting children and youth from the community because it was fun and was meeting their needs. The church school developed an expected pattern of response to the needs of the children in the community.

However, as it became more and more comfortable in its way of doing things, the system tended to close. It was typified by the statement, "That's just the way we do things here." As the attitudes closed, the ability of that church school to respond to new and emerging needs of the children in the neighborhood declined. Finally, fewer and fewer children came to the church school, because it was no longer meeting their needs. This was vividly expressed when Eric, who had always been in the church school class, got up enough courage to tell his parents and his church school teacher that he wasn't going to come back the next week. The teacher called on him at home after he had missed three or four weeks of classes and she put enough pressure on him that he came back. By this time, however, three or four other children saw that Eric had left and they too got enough courage to follow him. Thus, the pattern of deviancy from the expected norm of attendance began to build. The organization responded to this deviancy by setting up procedural rules and secondary rewards for attendance—pins and awards. However, the fact remains that Eric's basic needs were not being met, and secondary rewards became the reason for his being there even though he may have disliked the class.

The secondary reward means of dealing with deviancy tends to be dysfunctional, anticreative, or sinful. It is dysfunctional because it signifies alienation from the fundamental purposes of the organization. As the organization's purposes and goals get out of touch with the needs of the people whom they were designed to serve, alienation between that organization and its constituency grows. Alienation usually means that people simply lose interest in the voluntary organization and leave. In some organizations, however, this is not an option. For example, in the public school system, a child must attend by community decision whether or not the child finds it useful to his or her needs. In this situation, alienation has emotional manifestations that can cause significant conflict, particularly if it is shared by a large minority of the constituents. Conflict can signify a period of significant crisis in a dysfunctional organization. During this crisis stage, if the creative forces continue to feel alienated from the present organizational style, the organization will continue to decline. If the organization moves to a more open pattern and adjusts itself in such a way that it can respond to the newly emerging needs of the people, it will once again begin to grow. However, it is more likely that the conflict will be repressed and the organization will continue on a descending scale into a situation where there is total alienation from all creativity, resulting in a stubborn continuance by persons who want to protect the status quo. When this happens, the organization becomes an end in itself—it is dysfunctional and anticreative.

Psychological Dynamics

The dynamics of such an organization can be analyzed in terms of the psychological milieu, i.e., the roles that are played by the constituency, the role of myth and ideology and the psychic forces which are at work. The psychological milieu of an organization that is in decline is usually one of legalism, i.e., legalized formulas, stating how the organization retains its historic values. This ideology becomes crystallized without the esprit de corps which myth, belief, and attitudes represent. The dynamic factor produced by interaction between myth and reality is missing. The values that have come out of the experience of the organization while it was growing become institutionalized patterns of behavior. These are frequently made mandatory and in some cases become rituals. The institution proceeds to teach these patterns of behavior to all the constituency of that organization, but there is little meaning in the rituals for most of the participants. The next psychological stage is that of aimless wandering. The normative behavior pattern is designed for a situation that is no longer applicable because the situation has changed, so that there are no operational norms or values for the institution. When a state of aimlessness exists in an organization, the most likely result is alienation. Alienation is entirely dysfunctional to the life of an organization.

At the same time that this is occurring, new roles are being played by the constituency of the declining organization. These roles can be called the conservative, the rehabilitative, the revolutionary, and the reactionary roles. All of these roles are past-oriented. The persons in the constituency who play the conservative role attempt to preserve the values that originally gave rise to the organization even though they are no longer functional. In a religious organization this would be the person who tries to help the congregation hold on to the theological heritage that gave rise to that congregation. These persons not only try to reemphasize the values which gave rise to that church, but insist that the group reconstruct its historical heritage in the light of the denomination's founder, such as Wesley or Knox or Luther. For a conservative, the reconstruction of such values is more important than the preservation of the present system.

Others in the declining organization will tend to play the rehabilitative role. This role has little concern with the values of the past. Instead, the concern is with maintaining institutional machinery. The rehabilitative role player remembers the "good old days" when decisions were simple and directly made. There is no reason to have an administrative board, commission, or committee process. Do it as grandfather did it. The conservative role and the rehabilitative role vary only in degree. The conservative role places higher value on maintaining the values than it does on maintaining the system of the past. The rehabilitative role places more emphasis on maintaining the system of the past.

Other persons in the declining organization tend to play the revolutionary role. The revolutionary in an organization is an alienated conservative. The revolutionary almost never develops new values but rather selectively prioritizes past values. Since the existing system is unable to implement the priorities as he or she sees that they should be, the revolutionary becomes increasingly alienated from the organization. Finally, the only answer for the revolutionary is to leave or dissolve the organization.

Still others play the reactionary role. The reactionary role is the activist manifestation of the rehabilitative role. These persons are intensely committed to the system, but are alienated from its values. The system becomes an end in itself, and these persons militantly protect that system at all costs.

Creative Minority

Theologically and historically, however, there are additional dynamics at work that impinge upon the organizational life cycle and that must be taken seriously. At the same time that these processes of decline are proceeding, there is also a counterprocess at work. This counterprocess is represented by the creative minority. Every community and every civilization must have a creative minority if it is to remain a viable community or civilization. The hope is to identify them and mobilize them quickly.

When the organization is growing, the creative minority find the goals of the dominant organization not to be goals for them. Indeed, for them the organization's goals meet few of their perceived needs. Thus, there are a number of persons who very early in the process find themselves increasingly alienated from the basic goals of the organization. Their voice, however, is not usually heard. Rather, they emerge when the organization begins to decline and join in alliance with those who have become deviant from the declining organization. Sometimes, however, deviants are creative. They are sometimes the means of pumping creative alternatives into the life of an institution, which ultimately enables the institution to adjust. Frequently, however, the institution will continue to decline, because it will not adopt creative alternatives. When this happens, it is the creative minority who will develop the alternative organizations which enable the needs of the dominant populace to be met.

AGGRESSIVENESS AND PASSIVENESS IN ORGANIZATIONAL LIFE

For those few persons who have recently thought in the Oriental terms of the Yang and the Yin about organizations, the reasoning has been that when an organization is growing and aggressive, it is demonstrating its Yang characteristics. That same line of thinking would mean, if extended, that when an organization is at its effective plateau in its life cycle and then going into decline, it is less aggressive, and therefore the Yin characteristics dominate.

Perhaps the early philosophers can give us the clue to the real issue. The Eastern philosophers with their formulation of the Yin and the Yang and the followers of the Greek Empedocles with their understandings about periods of love and strife developed a concept of rhythm between the two ends of the spectrum. Essentially, they were saying that when the strife becomes excessive, the normal response is to lop over into the more passive style. When an organization begins to decline, the odds are very high that it will try to centralize decision-making. The social costs of centralized decision-making, however, are very great. As the organization moves further into decline, the likely alternative is that it will begin to follow the decentralized nonrational decision-making by individuals. This situation has occurred in the terminal stages of many previous organizations, communities, societies, and civilizations. Another tendency in a declining organization is to become increasingly specialized. In biological evolution, it is increasing specialization that makes a species less and less useful, and, finally, leads to its extinction. A successful direction of evolution has always been toward general indeterminism and cultural flexibility. The extreme use of institutional specialization to foster a specific quantitative growth in the life of the organization probably marks the approaching collapse of that organization. The only possible escape lies in the use of wholistic methods, turning the organization from a past orientation to a future generalized organization.

When an organization is in the growing stages of the life cycle, both Yin and Yang are at work as much as when it is in its declining stages of the life cycle. For example, a growing organization must have balance between the functions identified above as nurture and outreach. The nurturing phase has a great deal of similarity to the concepts of love and Yin. It is in this function that the group is nurtured to intensify relationships with one another in such a way that it may differentiate itself from the broader world. This nurturing provides the mutual respect and love that makes it possible for the organization to engage in its outreach functions. If the nurture and love become ends in themselves, the organization finds itself in trouble. But the opposite is also true. When the organization is engaged only in task and outreach, which are more aggressive and strife-ridden functions, and if it does not spend the time to develop its internal strength, it also finds itself in trouble. Thus the two forces must be kept in balance to have a viable organization.

It has traditionally been argued that when an organization is in decline, both of these forces are probably being misused and misdirected, to the detriment of the organization; the reactionary and revolutionary roles are aggressive roles but they are utilized to create strife that disintegrates the organization. The conservative and rehabilitative roles are more passive, but they too are misdirected, to the detriment of the organization. They are passive but nonetheless anticreative roles.

A case can be made, however, for a rhythm between the dominance of Yang and Yin in terms of leadership style at different times and as an organization moves through its life cycle. An organization that is growing usually has a very aggressive or Yang leadership style. But after the initial stages of growth, that charismatic and aggressive leadership style gives way to a style that can consolidate its gains. But it must be done in such a way that the organization develops a kind of wholeness of interaction between the maintenance and nurturing tasks, as the organization begins to come to a plateau and move into decline. It is quite normal for it to move into a more collaborative and bureaucratized leadership style. This style has more of the Yin characteristics. But by the time the organization goes into serious decline, the predominant leadership style is an affirmation of the past, and is frequently led by persons who are very aggressive in the affirmation of the past. And even the creative minority who find themselves increasingly excluded from the organization become very aggressive in their mood. Thus there is a rhythm between Yang and Yin— the organization tends to move from aggressiveness to collaboration and back to aggressiveness again. The difference is that the initial aggressiveness is creative, and the terminal aggressiveness is disintegrative. Thus, as in all of creation, these two roles interact for the mutual good in the creative stages, but they also interact for their mutual detriment in the disintegrative stages of organizational life. Nonetheless, no organization can be whole unless these two roles are in interaction.

Chapter VI

LEADERSHIP: ITS NATURE

IN THE DEVELOPMENT of churches and other organizations, the role of leaders is crucial. How people interact with their group, guiding and directing, has a vital effect on the life of the organization. It is essential to understand the nature of leadership if we are to understand organizations.

Leadership is an amorphous concept. Recently in the church as well as in other organizations, such as the Future Farmers of America, the Future Homemakers of America, and the 4-H Clubs, leadership had to do with speaking effectively in extemporaneous fashion and running an orderly meeting. Yet there probably is little correlation between these skills and being a leader generally. The church, like most other organizations that utilize professional leaders, has adopted standards of minimal training for leaders. The assumption is that if people meet these minimum standards, they are prepared to function as leaders. Yet there are extremely well trained ministers who are unsuccessful in leading congregations.

A similar situation exists among lay leaders of the church. In the Christian education arena, we have long offered "leadership training." It might more appropriately be called "skill training." Just because a lay person has

gone through his or her denominational leadership training activities, that person will not necessarily emerge as a
leader.

What is leadership then, and how does it function in an
organization or a congregation? Historically, leadership
refers to two different, but related, phenomena. One form
of leadership comes with position. That is, certain positions, or roles in society, have been set aside for leaders.
Sometimes these roles are formally inherited, as in English
royalty; or more informally inherited, as in the "leading
family" of a small rural community.

Some formal leadership roles are also assigned professionally. For example, there is a formal role in most communities called "the Superintendent of Schools." A person
from the outside is usually brought into this position because of his or her credentials and skills. The person is
expected to be the planner for the educational segment of
the community. Eventually, that person may earn the opportunity to be an influential pacesetter in the general
community life.

The pastor of a congregation in most American denominations is also in a professional leadership position. He or
she has met the denomination's requirements for the role
of congregational leader. These usually include educational requirements, experience under supervision of a
senior member of the profession, demonstration of personal spiritual maturity, and the approval of peers. With
these qualifications the clergyperson is then sent, assigned
or called—as an outsider—to be the pastor of a church
comprised of persons whom the pastor does not know.
These persons previously unfamiliar with each other must
then begin to develop the relationships that can be mutually helpful, but with the very real risk that the relationship may be or become mutually harmful. Similar situations exist with all community professionals, including
teachers, social workers, medical professionals, and busi-

ness leaders. The unique characteristic of this type of professional role is that it brings a person from outside, on the basis of credentials, to function as a leader. The leader has formal or professional credibility with the persons with whom he or she is to work.

A second leadership role is one accorded a person by his or her peers. For example, Martin Luther King, Jr., was chosen by his black church peers in Birmingham, Alabama, to lead them in dealing creatively with a very oppressive situation. He emerged from the group. Authority was accorded to him by the group, because he was able to choose the direction that seemed to them to be the only practical way. Most voluntary organizations begin with this type of leadership. Most of the "social change movements" are built around this type of leadership, and so are many congregations that resemble sects. It is leadership that results from a combination of the charismatic ability of a person to gather resources and the privilege accorded that person by the many who share the same needs.

Either way, whether the leadership role is formal or informal, the question still remains: What characteristics enable certain persons to work in the role described as leader in an organization?

THEOLOGICAL VIEWS

Leadership is one of the roles played in the effective organization. Yet leadership is often seen in hierarchies, like organizations. How often have we seen a triangle representing members of an organization with the top tip of that triangle shaded to represent its leaders? This image is one of hierarchy. It indicates that a certain percentage of the persons at the top function as an elite for the broader base of membership who are depicted as those at the bottom of the organization. This is not at all unlike the hierarchical organizational charts by which bureaucratic relationships are described, with each person answering to the person who is his or her superior, immediately above. This view implies that everything at the bottom exists for the top. This sort of organizational and leadership model did not happen accidentally. It has its roots in our theological view of reality. The churches have seen God as being "up there." They have seen the pope as the "vicar of Christ" sitting at the pinnacle of the hierarchy, and the bishops as intermediaries between them and the pope. This model was similar to the model developed by the Roman government with emperor and governors. It is also very closely related to the monarchical style of government. Religious practice and the way people organize the world imply that the bottom exists for the top. When the universe is seen as a three-storied reality—i.e., heaven, earth, and hell—an analogue of this model of leadership becomes evident.

God is no longer believed to be "up there," but rather, people are beginning to realize that God is "within and without." If God is not "up there," but is "in people," and if people participate with God in creation, the very nature of our understanding of leadership is changed, in the church as well as in society generally. It means that leadership is a role not only derived from the people but, more important, accorded to a person by the people. Authority is dispersed throughout the system. If God is in each of us, then we all have gifts and insights to share. Leadership becomes a role of liberating those gifts for the mutual benefit of all.

Perhaps no religious body has more distinctly defined leadership roles than the Roman Catholic Church. Yet recent experience indicates that even there, leadership can be derived from the people. A Catholic lay woman who was concerned that she did not know her Protestant neighbors invited several of them to her home for coffee. A morning coffee group developed and began to explore the differences and similarities in the faith and practices of their churches. Wanting to share with their children their commonly held beliefs, they planned a neighborhood Bible school, and then recruited the teachers and developed the organization. They told their various pastors that the first grade would meet in the Christian church, the second grade would meet in the Nazarene church, the third grade in the Catholic church, the fourth grade in the Presbyterian church, and so forth. The Bible school was a tremendous success, with more than seven hundred children enrolled for a two-week period. At the conclusion of the Bible school, these women were so joyous at what they had been able to do together in the name of Christ that they decided the best way to celebrate their joy was to join together in the Eucharist. They persuaded their pastors, including the Roman Catholic priest, to join them. The lay woman, her priest, and her bishop later indicated the importance of this event. The woman was able to celebrate commonality with others in the faith. Her priest cooperated, without requesting the bishop's permission, because he realized the invitation came from an authentic relationship which these people had developed with one another as persons of common faith. The Catholic bishop felt no compulsion to punish the priest for not asking permission, because what was going on in the community seemed appropriate, if not in terms of church law, at least in terms of authentic faith practice. Further, to have opposed that particular act might well have created a situation in which he would have lost influence in his community. This experience shows that leadership and authority are the product of mutual and interacting consent. Thus, increasingly, even in a hierarchical organization such as the Roman Catholic church, leadership results from interaction rather than from position.

Leadership of this sort flows from a more egalitarian view of humankind. It has probably emerged because of the equalizing effect of education and communication, as well as the broadened middle class which equips more persons for participation in decision-making and leadership. This means that people at each level in the church or in any other organization are making their own decisions rather than taking direction from above. When such creative interaction occurs, no one group or person is in charge and what does happen is less manipulatable by a few. Furthermore, authority or leadership in the traditional sense is modified. The proposed action occurs because it is authentic to the experience of the group. Little need is felt to check with anyone else. These trends stand in conflict with hierarchical church leadership styles that have their origin in another historical era. From that perspective, the emerging pattern seems less orderly; yet the emerging style of leadership has potential for participatory democratic order. Leadership is given by people to a person or a group of persons.

Hierarchy as a principle seems to have preceded the rise of the living religions, although religion became one of its main carriers. It probably goes back to the very nature of evolution on this planet: the survival of the fittest made hierarchy endemic to human experience. The strongest became the leaders. Yet, with the maturing of the social dimension of creation, it may be an idea that need not persist.

There are examples of attempts at order other than hierarchy in our political and religious history. For example, many aboriginal tribes have organized themselves collegially and worked by consensus. The Old Testament experiment with judges was also a move away from traditional hierarchy toward a form of collegiality. It did not work because of the peoples' demand for a king so they could be more like the other nations that surrounded them. Yet the move of Israel back to a kingdom was probably a regression from social innovation to a more traditional form—a regression which the biblical history indicates was fraught with problems for the "chosen people."

Other world religions, such as Buddhism and Hinduism, have had elements of hierarchy but have been at times more introspective and reflective than Christianity. They have sensed that God is within and consequently have not developed the leadership hierarchies characteristic of the Christian West and to a lesser degree Judaism and Islam.

Theologically speaking, Christianity has defined leadership from the person of Christ. Many have considered his role to be that of King, but the role of Christ seems better understood as being a prototype for all the community. Christ is the embodiment or the incarnation of the Torah and the Word. Christ is the embodiment and personification of the underlying creative will inherent in creation. In this sense, the personification becomes the prototype or the embodiment of what the Christian community should be. It dramatizes the possibility inherent in the creation for all humankind to be participants in that ongoing creativity. In some sense this is what incarnation implies. The person, Jesus, became the embodiment of the divine purpose, that is, became the prototype human—the Christ. That incarnation does not make Christ less or more human, but rather served to bring the divine purpose into focus in one human being at a specific time in history. This means that Christ not only was the source of God's original creativity but also emerged from that creativity as a part of the creation. Creator and creation are one. Therefore the advent of Christ in history dramatizes to the rest of humankind the possibilities that each possesses to be creator and created at the same time, to participate fully in the ongoing creation, by fulfilling our humanity as the created, with the Creator, in the ongoing work of creation.

Therefore, an authentic leader is a prototype in the sense that he or she, as created being, embodies the ideal of the group—other created beings—from which the leader has emerged to help the group liberate their energies and gifts so they can continue their mutual creative tasks. In the societal context, that person becomes the symbol of the potential which that group has of interacting with the remainder of society. The leader in an organization, like Jesus, demonstrates the possibility for the wholeness of relationship between that organization and the rest of society. He or she becomes a symbol of the possibility which is inherent in that organization and in the creation.

Probably the principal role any leader plays—beyond the symbolic one—is that of teacher or nurturer. Christ pointed the direction and possibility for humankind's participation in the broader arenas of creation but also accorded the privilege of being the teacher, or of helping people understand what these possibilities meant. This nurturing role is not one that comes from external authority, but rather it is one that comes from the very integrity of Christ. And so it is with any leader. Out of the integrity and quality of what he or she is, that person is accorded the privilege of being the teacher or the nurturer of other persons who look to that person because of his or her wholeness. In that sense, leadership is not simply an exercise of power, but rather, becomes a role model. It is the paradigm of what the potential is for the creation.

The models of leadership inherent in Christianity are not static. Christianity is dynamic. In the broad sense, leadership assists the group to move toward maturity in the context of the human situation. Moses made that possible for Israel even as Peter did for the church. Now as people come to a more egalitarian life-style and begin to realize that hierarchy may result in destructive competition, conflict, and alienation, there is no reason why they cannot grow beyond traditional interpretations of organization and the leadership roles in them. When the Christ event is seen as the personification of the Creator's creative will permeating the creation, rather than as dominating over the creation, the mode of thinking about incarnation changes. This mode of thinking has biblical foundations. In the Old Testament, it is evident in much of the Torah teachings. In the New Testament, it is evident in much of Jesus' teaching about the Kingdom that is within people.

Unfortunately, in our churches and our society people cling to the hierarchical bureaucratic leadership styles—even when democratically chosen. Bureaucracies are often inefficient, unjust, and dehumanizing, yet people do not like the alternatives such as the inherited power of monarchy, absolute dictatorships, and socialist committee rule. But as people mature they will have to transcend these alternatives, be socially inventive, and give social form to those heretofore unexplored possibilities for leadership which are inherent in our faith. The person interacting with the group will be an essence of these new forms.

COMPONENTS OF LEADERSHIP

The potential for leadership is a gift—a capacity. Persons are born with certain capacities. Society then helps. As the person interacts with society, community, or organization, these capacities develop into what might be described as charisma. (This may be seen as an energy exchange between person and organization—"good vibes," a propensity to become the prototype for the organization.) Charisma is a gift which the individual brings to the organization. In the New Testament, persons were spoken of as having the gift of prophecy, the gift of teaching, the gift of preaching, etc. Thus, charisma comes from the interaction between a person's native ability and the socialization which nurtures those abilities to meet the needs of the broader community. But to become a charismatic leader requires still a third element: the historically significant moment. When innate ability interacts with the organization, the congregation, or the society, which in turn interacts with a crucial need—the historically significant moment—the person can emerge who is accorded the privilege of leading a whole group of persons. That person is said to be charismatic. There are numerous examples in history of the ways in which this combination has worked. The apostle Paul, for example, was obviously a capable person with many innate abilities. Although a Jew, he was raised in the Hellenistic traditions of the Greco-Roman culture. Undoubtedly he could have been a successful teacher or public servant. At the time of his conversion, however, he underwent a radical reorientation of his values which meant that he chose to serve Christ whom he perceived to be the Son of God. He was present at the historic and appropriate moment when the young church was facing a crisis of direction. Because of his abilities and his background, he was able to help the young church "turn the corner" from being a subdivision of Jewish culture to interacting creatively with the Hellenistic and Roman culture. Thus, Paul was given the opportunity by the young church, despite conflict, of becoming a charismatic leader pointing the direction for the organization's creative involvement in the dominant culture.

Similar illustrations could be developed in relation to many of the great leaders of the church, including Augustine, Peter Waldo, Martin Luther, John Wesley, John Calvin, John Knox, and Martin Luther King. Each had innate abilities. Each had his abilities sharpened through interaction with the broader society and the religious situation of which he was a part. At some point in the life of each of these persons, their perceptions of reality and their vision of what should be were sharpened much as Paul's was on the Damascus road. This experience, coupled with the historical situation in which they found themselves, thrust them forth as charismatic leaders for a large segment of the church of their time. The charismatic leader is a gift to society—to promote the needed creativity at a crucial moment in the history of the church or society.

However, not many are accorded the privilege of becoming the creative and charismatic leaders. Rather, most people are expected to cultivate their native abilities to the utmost in order to contribute in a variety of less dramatic ways to the ongoing development of their organizations and society. If leadership is a gift of the people to a person, in a very real sense, charisma is a gift of the person to the people. The extent to which the leader will be able to share that gift with the people depends to a large extent upon the leader's sense of wholeness and identity. In this sense each person's ability to make order out of some small pieces of the chaos in which he or she lives, through teaching, preaching, counseling, prophecy, or administration, is a gift to the whole creation. Each person has gifts to share and contribute.

Unfortunately, traditional patterns of hierarchy in the church and the society often violate the integrity of what a person has to share. In a hierarchical organization people tend to share only those gifts which the next higher person in the organization is willing to receive. In this way the majority of a person's gifts are unavailable to the organization. This fact in turn limits many creative possibilities and impedes the ongoing development required for greatest participation in the creation. The sort of hierarchical organization which all people experience daily in their work actually conditions them to "keep their place," "do their little task," and "not offer more than is wanted." Too often "more" threatens "superiors" because it questions their control. "More" also brings pressure for mediocrity from peers, because it makes them look bad.

BARRIERS TO LEADERSHIP

There are many personal factors, however, which become barriers to creative participation as leaders. Personality itself may be a problem. For example, Paul required a radical reorientation of values on the Damascus road through a conversion experience to enable him to understand who he was in the context of the total creation. This was a freeing experience which released him from many of the internal conflicts that frequently immobilize people. In this experience, he found a wholeness which caused him to contribute his significant gifts to the ongoing creation. Although many do not experience this radical reorientation of values, nonetheless, unless they come to a personal sense of wholeness and belonging in the whole realm of creation—i.e., at-one-ment with the creation—their ability to contribute will be extremely limited. Persons who are at war with themselves have little ability to participate creatively in an organization or in the broader arenas of society.

There are numerous biblical examples of what happens when those who are accorded leadership are themselves in conflict. Exodus 3 and 4 describe Moses' conflict over accepting leadership of Israel and leading the people from bondage in Egypt. Another vivid example of one refusing leadership because of conflict was Jonah. What he wanted to do and what he knew he should do were in tension. Until the conflict was resolved he was unable to lead. Another illustration is Gideon, whose fears made him hide in the winepress rather than lead, as God insisted.

Besides personality conflicts, entanglements such as competition and self-assertion at others' expense form barriers which impede persons from utilizing their charisma effectively in behalf of Creator and creation. All organizations are political in the sense that whenever two or more persons are interacting, there is always a certain amount of rivalry for position. In complex organizations these moves for advantageous position can take on significant implications. They can become effective barriers to creative participation, leadership, or contribution to the ongoing life of that organization. Compromise, which in a cooperative way leads to a creativity that exceeds the sum of the parts, is good for the organization. This is called a win-win situation. But compromise is not usually of this kind. We often play a win-lose game. The winner gets control and the loser is subjugated, with his or her gifts lost to the group or with the person reduced to an opposition role.

The win-lose game for leadership is a barrier, because it is based upon an assumption that power and control are total, and to be a leader one must control as much of that totality as possible. Most people would reject this variation on the dictator's style of leadership. It is also based on a misunderstanding of the "survival of the fittest" theme in evolution. Leadership that emerges on the basis of these two assumptions will impede the creative possibilities inherent in organization for the following interrelated reasons:

1. Communication will decline, isolating the winner from the group. Control by one person of many reduces the interaction between leader and group mostly to experiences of oppression and pain. People tend to avoid such pain, and not communicate.

2. The organization is limited to the gifts, policies, and psychic resources of the winner. The losers' gifts and resources not only are not made available by them but usually are actively repressed by the winner.

3. What energy the losers do have is usually directed toward a strategy of toppling the winner, rather than contributing to the overall purposes of creativity—i.e., resources are absorbed within.

Contemporary understandings of group and organizational dynamics are showing that assumptions are wrong about the power and survival of the fittest. Power is not a complete commodity which must diminish if shared with another person. The nature of creation seems to demonstrate that power is infinitely expandable. It is only limited by people's unwillingness to be open and give what they have to others and receive in return. With the "survival of the fittest" the species that succeeded were those which were adaptable to the changing environments, not those which could fight best in the old environment. The most effective and specialized fighters in the old environment were the species that became extinct. Thus, win-win interaction can be creative, but win-lose activity in a congregation, an organization, or a society becomes a barrier to personal, organizational, and societal creativity. It can become overtly destructive to the organization and it drains energy and the ongoing creativity which an organization requires.

Closely related to this is the barrier related to the organization's life cycle and history. Some organizational leaders have a nineteenth-century style when the times and the organization demand a more contemporary approach. To bring to an organization gentlemanly elitism appropriate to the nineteenth century is inappropriate to the contemporary pluralistic organizational requirements of the present. Such a leadership style can become a barrier to creativity.

Thus, persons as a natural product of God's creation, and as a social product of their environment, have the opportunity to cultivate their charisma as a gift to the organization in broader society. When this is done, a wholeness emerges, and a contribution is made to the creative focusing of the creation. At the same time, however, there are many external factors in the life of the institution and society which determine whether or not that contribution is utilized creatively, or whether it plays into the hands of the anticreative forces, which are always at work in society.

Chapter VII

LEADERSHIP: ITS FUNCTION

MANY MINISTERS and lay people have been consumed by their role as church leaders. They seem to be carrying all the work on their backs. They are unable to share the responsibility and ultimately they "burn out."

One pastor was assigned a particularly difficult small-town charge and was told by his bishop that this was a make-or-break charge for him professionally. If he did well, he would undoubtedly be assigned a significantly larger church in a few years; if not, he would probably spend the rest of his ministry in uninteresting situations. The pastor's reaction to the ultimatum was to undertake that ministry in a manner quite out of keeping with his previous basic rather collaborative style of ministry. But now he developed a great need to control everything that went on in the parish.

By the end of the second year things were booming. There were more activities and good things happening for the members than ever before. In the third year the burden and tension became too great and the pastor broke— with deep stress-related emotional problems and a heart attack. He recovered physically, but he is still an emotionally burned out person struggling to find the wholeness he once knew.

His experience overlooked a basic tenet about the function of leadership in an organization. Organizational and church leadership is the coalescence of professional and volunteer leaders in such a way that their combined work points toward wholeness within the organization, and in turn leads that organization toward its creative role in the larger society. When this happens, the individual is not consumed by the organization, but both the person and the organization are creatively fulfilled by the interaction of their leadership. It is through the organization that the leader is able to express her or his wholeness and participation in the broader society.

Organizational leadership is a paradox, however. As indicated earlier, leadership is not merely the exercise of power in the organization, but rather is paradigmatic. The leader is a prototype or representative of the best hopes of the organization. That is, the organizational leader symbolically celebrates the power of the people, inherent in the underlying myth or values that gave rise to the organization in the first place. Yet even though the leader is the symbol of the myth and dream, he or she is also called upon to transcend those dreams of the past and to point to the future. This is something of a tightrope-walking act. The leader must stay on the tightrope while extending with one hand back into the past, holding on to the original myth and dream that gave rise to the organization, and affirming the constituency of the organization in those dreams and myths. At the same time, the other hand must be reaching uncertainly into the future and pointing the direction by which it is possible for the constituency of that organization to transcend the limitations of the past and creatively participate in the future.

The difficulty of this task is even more intense in an era of cooperative leadership. Formerly strong leadership was appreciated in pointing the direction and telling people what to do. But many capable people in churches and groups often become very wary of strong leaders. Egalitarian organizations and charismatic leaders have blocked each other. Consequently many organizations lose energy for a creative common life. Such energy might have resulted from interaction of individual perspectives, with mutual trust, confidence, and organizational styles. The liberation of participants in organizations has sometimes weakened potential leaders: no one is able to set the direction of the group. The result is organizational drift. What this era desperately needs is to find the way for strong participatory organizations to utilize the skills of their most effective leaders in such a way that they can transcend this tension in reaching a new level of creativity.

LAY LEADERSHIP AND PROFESSIONAL LEADERSHIP

At no point is this tension more powerfully revealed than in the problems of conflict that often arise between professional leadership in an organization and the voluntary leadership. The theory in many organizations was that professional leadership was to devote full time to implementing the tasks which the voluntary leadership in the organization outlined. For example, in the school systems of our country professional teachers and professional administrators came into existence as a resource to assist the voluntary leadership of the community in a task they felt important to carry out, that of the education of their children. Sometimes formerly creative professional leadership becomes conservative and counterproductive leadership in the present. The professional establishment, in many areas of community life, may have grown so strong that there is little opportunity for the voluntary leadership to wrest the control out of its hands. Frustration is felt by both the professional and the voluntary leaders. That frustration tends to lead to organizational and societal apathy and a sense of helplessness.

Among the churches, in the static Roman Catholic Church prior to Vatican II all the decisions about the organization were made by the professional leaders of that church, with no significant influence from the lay constituents. This situation has now been significantly modified, but in the Roman Catholic churches, as well as in most of the Protestant communions, the balance of power still rests with those who are professionally related to the church. Therefore, they frequently make decisions that may not be in the interest of the broader organizational goals or purposes of those churches. For example, the laity of the churches have frequently demonstrated a pragmatic ecumenism by attending whatever church is most convenient to them. Yet many clergy continue the "conspiracy of denominationalism" by developing loyalty to the denomination first and only incidentally to the church universal. Further, those lay persons who do rise to the positions of leadership within the denominational church frequently are those who have learned to play the denominational game better than their peers. This gamesmanship has caused clergy to recommend them for leadership because they represent the interests of the professionals. When this happens, there may be little ability among the professional or the voluntary leaders to deal creatively with emerging needs. There is no serious criticism or dialogue in the organization and it winds up with a very conserving stance rather than an innovative one.

There is still another aspect to the professionalization process which affects organizations. A profession exists by building boundaries. People have to meet certain minimum requirements before they can be accepted into the professional "club." Even after those requirements are met, the "club" still usually must take a vote to decide whether or not to accept them. Frequently, the requirements have to do as much with professionalism self-interest as with the interest of the organization that they were designed to serve. A professor friend used to say that each time the church raised the educational standards of its clergy, it wound up writing off a segment of the population with whom the less well trained clergymen were capable of communicating. This is to say that when the professional standards of the organization become too sophisticated, the professionals are trained so they have little ability to communicate with those who represent other socioeconomic and political values in the organization. Consequently, others' needs are not fulfilled, and they drift away from that church and become approachable by the sect movements.

A related problem is that even though a person has met the minimum requirements for entrance into the "professional club," that fact still does not mean that he or she will be a leader. How many persons with professional credentials in education, social work, government, law, politics, or in the church, are incapable leaders? They may have emerged from the group, they have been certified by the professionalization processes of the group, but that still does not guarantee that they can command the respect of the constituency. This may be for the lack of innate ability, but more likely it has to do with the barriers discussed in Chapter VI, or the inability of the organization really to trust that person.

The interaction between professional leadership and voluntary leadership required to make an organization "go" is often difficult. Each seems an uneven match for the other. Yet, through collective interaction between professional and lay leadership, it is possible to transcend the limitations of either, and build an open interaction which enables the organization to be creative and progressive. Such models are emerging and are being developed, as will be seen in the concluding parts of this chapter.

LEADERSHIP AND ORGANIZATIONAL DYNAMICS

However, other factors related to the dynamics in organization which impinge upon leadership and staffing styles will be explored first. One of these is the organizational life cycle described above. The roles played by members of an organization vary significantly as the organization goes through its several stages of growth, golden mean, and finally decline. But the style of professional leadership must also vary significantly depending upon the institutional stage. When an organization is on the growing part of the scale, the role of the professional staff, as well as the voluntary leadership, is charismatic. It is the task of the professional staff to help the organization develop and focus the myths about reality so that more and more people can respond. The leader must help the constituency to dream and build motivational myths. After the mythologizing task is done, the leader must help the group translate those myths, dreams, and fantasies into actualized goals for action. Thus, when an institution is in an ascending role, leadership functions in a charismatic fashion, catching the imagination and giving direction to that organization.

When organizational growth levels off and it approaches the golden mean, the role of professional leader begins to change. At this point the charismatic role gives way to a symbolic and management role. The myth has become formalized into an ideological belief pattern. Tradition becomes more important, and the roles played by the lay leadership shift from the feeling, intuitive, pragmatic, and synthesizing roles to the conservative, rehabilitative, revolutionary, or reactionary roles. When the organization moves too far down the descending scale, it usually means that the professional leader becomes the custodian of the formalized and crystallized past. Innovative leadership is not trusted. Yet if leadership is to be creative, it must help the organization redream its reason for being, and find new directions for its life.

EMERGING MODELS OF LEADERSHIP

To be sure, the roles of leadership are changing in the organizations in our Western culture, because our needs and our perceptions of reality are changing. The emerging models and patterns of leadership in organizations will also be changing significantly. This situation affects both leadership style and leadership role in the organization, particularly as they relate to the professional person. It would seem that several styles of leadership that will have importance for the future are currently emerging. The first of these might be called the collegial or the shared leadership model. As the difference and the distance between the professional leader and the constituency become less, increasingly the organizational system opens. Status becomes less important, and persons are accepted for what they are and what they can contribute to the group. This fact means that leadership is increasingly shared. Goals are developed out of the group's needs and their perceptions of the community's issues. Group members join task groups that interest them, to implement the goals they feel to be the most important for the organization. Each task group's accountability is to the whole group rather than to a leader or staff person. This means that the leadership role of the professional is increasingly that of a facilitator, enabler, and synthesizer rather than an accountable administrator in the traditional hierarchical and bureaucratic sense of accountability. It also means that the professional leader stands with the people and together they participate in the ongoing creation. Therefore, professional leaders are entering into team relationships with their lay peers quite apart from the traditional status considerations. They become mutually supportive of each other and find fulfillment together in team relationships, as opposed to individual success. Here is a significant illustration. After the merger of two denominations, individual congregations could choose for governance either a prescribed plan or one they developed. One church, led by a pastoral team and a consultant, rethought their values in ministry. They identified several, including: (1) the "priesthood of all believers" and its requirements for shared ministry; (2) the facilitative role of the pastoral team; (3) the maintenance of the organization by laity—but only by a few as their stewardship which would free the majority for ministry; (4) the importance of people using their gifts and skills for the ministries that interested them the most; (5) the importance of nurture as a process for youth and adults; and (6) the importance of actively working for the wholeness of the emerging suburban community.

Then, they developed a series of goals they wanted to realize over the next five years in the church fellowship and in the community. The task was then to develop congregational structure, or form, so it could act upon these agreed-upon values and goals.

Their model also incorporated many important but subordinate values, such as the integration of the adult faith learning with experience and focus of human resources, so that no person should have two tasks before each person had one task.

The result of this planning was a creative model for channeling the congregation's energy for mutual nurture and mutual outreach.

At the end of the first year, organizational maintenance —including building maintenance, stewardship drives, membership assimilation, and management of the business affairs—was being done by a half dozen persons, thus freeing 594, theoretically, for other creative forms of ministry. A coordinating team of nine had oversight of all congregational nurture. Three gave specific oversight to children and youth nurture. Three had responsibility for family nurture and fellowship. Three others worked with the pastors in the development of meaningful worship and music experiences.

The majority of the members, however, were involved in "Community Outreach" ministries. Initially, a dozen community concerns were identified. Up to forty persons could select a Study/Task Group working on one of these concerns. They chose their own leader and developed their own course of action under the facilitative guidance of a pastor. The goal was to make a difference in the community and at the same time understand the issue more fully themselves. The leaders served on the Community Outreach Coordinating Council and provided overall direction to the process. Three or four times a year the three teams of leaders from "Congregational Nurture," "Community Outreach" and "Organizational Maintenance," along with the pastors, met for communication and coordination.

The system worked well. It was collaborative; it liberated everyone's gifts; leadership was shared throughout. It had impact on the community. It encouraged and resulted in growth—of the members and in membership.

Then, a new pastor was assigned who was uncomfortable with the strangeness of the system. He needed to feel in control. Consequently he dismantled the creative experiment and reinstituted the prescribed system—probably at the suggestion of the ecclesiastical superiors who were also new and did not know how to deal with what they perceived to be an aberration. So this creative experiment in shared leadership came to an end.

The church is not the only place where there is experimentation with new styles of leadership. Collegial leadership styles are also emerging at some points in government, health care, and business, as well as in education and other aspects of the private sector. It is one of the directions for the future.

These collegial trends mean that leadership is "patterning" in styles that were unknown in the past. This patterning, as suggested in the model shared above, is occurring in at least three general areas. The first has to do with the creative minority. As suggested earlier, much of the creativity emerging within and among contemporary established organizations is the product of a creative minority within the life of the organization who have come together because of common concerns that are not being dealt with creatively in the organization. These experiences of working on common concerns led certain people to learn to trust each other. For example, one metropolitan council of churches had become very obsolete in programs and mode of operation. The organization was losing support. Some of the most frustrated voluntary leaders began to meet and dream some new dreams about the role of the churches in metropolitan areas. The group trusted one another and became convinced they had the responsibility to develop the strategy that would lead the organization in new directions—which they eventually were able to do, with a very creative result. This mutual energy for creativity gave the churches of the metropolitan region an organization that could respond to the needs which the minority had discussed. These patterns increasingly mean that initiative for organizational change may come from any place within the organization, and on occasion from any place in the community. Time was when people negotiated in political fashion to get the hierarchy to move. Now as responsibility is shared, initiatives may come from any place in the community system or in the organization system. "The initiative belongs to those who take it." The creativity of this style puts pressure on the old forms. If the custodians of the old do not respond, eventually the creative replaces the regressive.

The second patterning of leadership has to do with the dynamic coalitional or task force model. This model of leadership patterning is typified by people who, for one reason or another, come together around an issue of mutual concern. They work on that issue until it is solved. They give concerted leadership to that concern, but when the solution is reached, they disband to reconfigure around other issues. They do not create an ongoing organization. Apparently these persons work in a tertiary relationship with a creative minority. They are not controlled by those persons who give rise to an organization, but they do respond to those issues which converge with their self-interest, work until there is a solution, and then drift away.

Leadership patterning also is occurring in still a third way. It relates to peer grouping of professional leaders. People of similar background and responsibility seem to feel most comfortable together. Thus, grouping has become a common phenomenon of community organization leaders, the bishops of the various communions, business leaders, leaders of middle judicatories in the denominations, downtown pastors, neighborhood pastors, neighborhood business associations, etc. These groups are increasingly generating concern and insights, often overcoming emotional isolation of participants or developing special skills. The unfinished task of organization at this point is finding some way to link these peer groups in a creative fashion for the broader community's mutual benefit. The model shared above did not do this, so when the ecclesiastical superior changed and the pastor changed, permission to be innovative was withdrawn from the congregation.

What does all this say about the leadership style required by organizations in the future? Given the emerging style of decision-making in our society, which tends to be a negotiation model by which a number of self-interest groups discover their common agendas, the shared common agenda will become the basis of the voluntary institution of the future. It seems quite likely that professional leadership will increasingly have to become the enablers, facilitators, and synthesizers of this process. To the extent to which this occurs, it will be increasingly difficult for the "prima donnas" to find their way in the emerging society. Most of the collegial leadership models of the future will probably require that each individual bring some specialty to the total group. It will also require each person to become involved as a person in that group. The factors contributing to traditional professional status will be less important in this organizational style. Individual leaders will have to function in an egalitarian peer relationship.

Thus, the leader will be required to engage in mature egalitarian interaction with his or her peers, which will include both the professional and the voluntary persons involved in that organization. No longer would the traditional professional (parent), voluntary (child), relationship be tolerated—all are equal. It will be the role of both the professional and the volunteer leader to help that organization maintain some social boundaries, while at the same time helping the organization to thrust beyond those boundaries.

Leadership will be no less important in the future; only the ways in which it is played out in our society will change. We will still need strong leadership, but the style of leadership will be derived from the constituent organization in a fashion different from what it has been in the past. If we derive it in an open fashion, building patterns of interaction among the gifts that all the constituents of the organization have to bring and then liberating those gifts in a channeled direction, it will make impact upon the dominant society, nudging it toward wholeness and fulfillment.

Chapter VIII

FUTURE

THE DRAMATIC BIBLICAL IMAGE of the New Jerusalem as a transcendent city represents our faith and hope that creation will one day reach fulfillment and wholeness. In all its radiant beauty, it is in marked contrast to the void and desert of the origins described in Genesis. This fulfillment of the development of God's cosmos and human communities is the future goal. Discussion of patterns affecting leadership has provided glimpses of the emerging shapes of future organizational life. This present chapter will explore further the future shape of organizational life. It will also review basic premises of theology and creativity in creation. Much of the foregoing material is based upon theological and sociological assumptions of progress (e.g., history and human organization is developmental and is moving in a direction that will ultimately bring fulfillment to history). Yet questions remain. Have our organizations really moved us toward wholeness, or only toward more conflict, aggression, and war? Is there really progress, or not? What is in store in the future?

This final chapter will address the future shape of organizations. Can one know when organizations are functioning to help people to be participants in the creation, rather than oppressing them?

As seen earlier, history oscillates between Yin and Yang. Philosophers have also observed that civilization oscillates between subjective orientation and objective orientation. Since the initiation of the Christian era, and particularly since the Reformation, the predominant philosophical orientation of the Western world has been subjective. That is, it has given principal concern to the person. This major thrust in organizational style came to flower in the American Revolution of 1776 and the French Revolution which began in 1789. These revolutions were codified into constitutional agreements which gave the individual more freedom, liberty, and rights than had ever been known before in any civilization. These organizations were conceived to enhance the rights, privileges, and liberties of the individual. These organizational styles, with their bias toward the individual or the subjective orientation, were a major gift of Western culture to the whole world. Along with this gift came the organizational style known as democratic bureaucracy. Essentially, the rationale developed that through democratic assemblies people could make decisions about how to deal with their corporate needs. Because people's perceived needs were countless, it became impossible through voluntary means to deal with them, and one result was that bureaucracies were created to do for the people that which they did not have time or expertise to do for themselves.

Yet among the characteristics of bureaucracies is that they may eventually become self-serving, like any developed organization past its prime, and the result is inefficiency and a loss of individual freedom.

These problems and the needs of the future for new, just, and more creative ways to organize human participation in the creation provide the church with a significant challenge. In Western society the church has been a major carrier of subjective values. While it has advocated and maintained the value of the individual, it has been slow in assessing the perversion of those values in political and economic life. It has been slow to assert those values of the faith that argue the value of the objective—the group— values. The time has come when the church must seriously reassess its institutional role in the organizational hierarchy of Western cultural organization in a variety of ways. Normatively, the church, the "people of God," is called to be God's holy nation—the embodiment of the Torah or the Word, the embodiment of the creative impulse that gave rise to the creation in the first place. The "people of God" are to be the prototype in the community, the society, and the culture of God's intention for all creation. Although the church is a human organization, it is to be a human organization that embodies and dramatizes the hope of the Creator for the whole created order.

To the extent to which the church embodies the anti-creative propensities of the community, the society, or the culture toward hierarchy and competitive fragmentation, it has itself become unfaithful to its prototype role in creation. It is to be a sacrament for the rest of society, taking the stuff of creation and using it for the purposes of creation's fulfillment, i.e., transforming it as an act of hope and faithfulness. This does not mean that all the forces and dynamics of organizational life that are described above should not be at work in the church. It does mean that people of the church should be using God-given intellect and faith-given insight to the best of their ability, so the church can be more than just another organization.

If the church is to be renewed for its original purpose, it must reappropriate fundamental theological understanding inherent in its biblical origins, and build them into the center of its organizational life. Most important are the biblical understandings of: (1) creation as process or development; (2) covenant as a unique calling to the prototype role as sign and symbol of God's intention that creation might be whole; (3) collegiality, mutuality, egalitarianism, and interdependence, with their resulting liberation, rather than hierarchy, power, autonomy, and independence, with their competitive and oppressive waste of resources; (4) interdependence between the person and the community, rather than competition between them; (5) unity that comes from complementary diversity, rather than the debilitating fragmentation that comes from the pluralism of autonomous self-interests; and (6) call for atonement, harmony, Shalom, among all parts of the creation, rather than the appropriation by one segment of the creation of the majority of the whole creation's resources for its private benefit. In short, the church must embody those values which are in contradistinction to the tendencies of humankind to participate with the forces opposing creation. The very quality of the church as organization must be a qualitative call to the other dimensions of creation from sin to wholeness.

The church, as congregations in the community, as systems of congregations, called denominations, and as systems of systems which is the church universal, must demonstrate the future—beginning now. Christians, like Jews, are in a covenant relationship to fulfill their part as sacrament. Failure would mean that neither God nor people will be fulfilled, and there is always the possibility that the great experiment in creation could be lost—at least in terms of the segment of creation known as Earth. With this possibility, the agenda for God's people should be clear. Christians must deal with the crippling contradictions in our group life. Christians must open themselves to models of group life that are often quite contrary to what society now practices. Such models, like the one described in the previous chapter, are emerging on the growing edges of the church. The church must appropriate the best of those new experiences, or its prototype role in society—its mission—will be lost. The exact shape its future organization will take is unclear, but it must both develop and still incorporate biblical values.

What is true of the church is true in a different way in other organizations in society—political, economic, and educational. Styles can emerge that appropriate the best of the subjective, individualistic values in the Western world, the objective group-oriented values developed in the East, as well as the tribal and ecological values inherent in the third world. Organizational style in the future will require people to realize interdependence with one another and with the biosphere—the earth—as never before. Further, it will require people in the Western world to see personal liberties in the light of the needs of the whole group, while the communist second world and the emerging peoples of the third world will need to see the group in the light of individual needs and rights. Organization of society in the future will require new modes of mutuality in decision-making as well as new styles of implementation which are not elitist and not bureaucratic in nature. In addition, emerging organizational styles must find ways to share resources more equally, must find ways to provide for communication and collaboration between organizations at each level, as well as finding new ways to accept each person's contribution to the whole. Future organizations will have to function in a nonoppressive manner by moving away from the power politics now prevalent in Western, Communist, and the emerging third worlds. It may require new regional political structures to replace the present nation states and perhaps tribalism within those new regional arrangements.

In all probability, complex hierarchically organized societies will be forced to move from traditional bureaucratic structure toward more egalitarian and interactive ones. Ideally, each part of the organizational system of the future will have equal integrity. Each part will give to the whole and receive from the whole as it has need. If it contributes nothing, it will ultimately receive nothing, because if it is not useful to the whole, it will not receive support from the whole.

Does organizational life really progress in this way? Is there hope of moving to such an organization style? In the past five or six thousand years of recorded history, there have been few generations that have known peace. Persons were in conflict with each other, their tribes and organizations were in conflict, and their nations were at war. Is there any basis for a progressive understanding of organizational maturity? It should be noted that conflict does not necessarily mean lack of progress. In fact, it is the very nature of change to develop conflict. Unfortunately people have not been able to manage this conflict to reinforce their creativity. Rather, the conflict has frequently been used to reinforce the status quo.

Certainly the illusion of progress is evident in our technological development from the stone age to the nuclear era. Our transportation system has progressed from walking to rockets. Our communication techniques have moved from talking and storytelling to the still theoretical ability to transfer a person instantaneously from one place to another to communicate in person with anyone with whom he or she sees fit to talk. Further, communication now extends from the two-person pair, the family, or the tribe to the whole world via mass media techniques. The scale of organizations has been continually pushed upward from the family to the tribe to the city to the nation and to the world level, with the result that an ever-greater interdependence has been developed among all inhabitants of the earth. Less personal energy is now required for the person's survival, and more human energy can go into the arts, religion, and other things which build the human spirit. Horizons have been broadened. Awareness on the part of the individual in our society is perhaps as great today as it has ever been in the history of civilization. Yet, at the same time that our technology has made these gains possible, the way we have organized these gains lags behind. Organizational progress has been slower, but it has developed in much of the world to the benefit of more people.

So, even though there are organizationally dysfunctional aspects to many of the signs of progress, it would be difficult to argue that the last five thousand years have not shown significant societal movement, if not progress. For the optimist, progress seems to be both an empirical fact and a statement of faith.

It would seem, however, that there are some major insights to be developed in the way people organize life if they are to make the next leap from destructive conflict, which impedes overall progress, to constructive conflict which will transcend the present and reinforce progress. When we are able to accept the insights explored in the earlier chapters, civilization will be able to transcend itself and make the leap which the future requires. Therein will lie the new creativity which society desperately needs, and without which it will be impeded indefinitely.

The first essential insight to develop is that the quality of relationships in organizational systems is as important as the quality of the parts or the integrity of the parts in the system. For example, the reality of the family is every bit as important as are the father, mother, son, and daughter. It is something that transcends those four persons. So it is with every organization. Until people realize this, they will be incapable of dealing creatively with organizational life. An example lies in the church. Denominations have denied when they come together in ecumenical council that the meeting is the church. Yet the New Testament itself says, "Where two or three are gathered in my name, there am I," implying that the church is there. Yet each part of the church, whether congregation or the community or denominations in council, has often maintained that it is sovereign. The same can be said for the nations in the United Nations. Essentially, they have denied, by their actions, that the United Nations is any more than the sum of its parts. Each part maintains that it is sovereign. This has impeded the development of whole relationships. Because of this, it has been difficult for the United Nations to be an effective force of world interdependence. It might be noted that a similar circumstance presented itself at the time of the Constitution in the United States, between the "states' rights persons" and those who felt that the republic should be more than the sum of the parts of the states. That issue continued through the Civil War, and to this present day impedes the wholeness of the nation.

The second essential insight is closely related to the first. That is, just because an organization is more than the sum of its parts, it cannot violate its parts. The secret of this lies in understanding the real meaning of mutuality. To be sure, to be a part of an organization means to submit some autonomy to the whole—one gives up some things. But more important, people bring gifts to the whole, and even more important, are enriched by the gifts others bring. The result is that people transcend as a whole what they are as parts, not only to their mutual benefit but to the benefit of the larger community. The collaboration and its resulting "synergism" exceeds the sum of the parts. It transcends, but does not violate the parts.

This idea leads to a third insight. If society is to make the leap into a creative future, it must move away from competitive, win-lose politics to a collaborative style where the creativity of each part is taken into equal consideration. The win-lose politics of the last six thousand years of recorded history probably is only a stage in societal development. People are only now really learning that there is a win-win alternative that can transcend the toleration and cooperation that come from self-interest alone. Cooperation and toleration are better values than the stronger destroying the weaker, but they can be only sophisticated and controlled forms of profound disdain and hatred based on power balances. Win-win styles move an organization or a society closer to total acceptance, if not authentic love for that which is different. It transcends power needs.

Finally, the organizational styles of the future will require people to use conflict creatively in the form of energy to reinforce progress. People are learning on a limited scale from group dynamics how to do this with small and moderately complex groups. They have not, however, learned how to do this with more sophisticated and complex groups at metropolitan, state, national, and world levels. Nor do people use what they know in business, religion, politics, or education. If they could channel half of the energy exerted on infighting to more creative activities, how rapid the changes could be!

Therefore, Christians still live with the hope and anticipation that through their organizational life, humankind can participate with the Creator in the ongoing creation; that we can, in fact, move from a static and oppressive organizational style to a truly creative organizational style. Christians must make no apology for that hope. Further, they must learn that organizations are dynamic and alive. They can be creative or they can destroy themselves from within. But renewal or healing is always a possibility—if not the probability. Revolution is one form of possible renewal, for example. It may expel the cancer that is eating away in the life of the organization. But revolution is like major surgery. It seeks to cure sometimes at great cost to the patient. Therefore there must be more efficient ways than revolution to deal with the need for organizational change. There is an alternative which people are only beginning to see—some have called it "provolution." Provolution is planned, rapid revolution which, instead of excising the cancer by surgery, removes it through a healing process, making whole. In addition to trying to reform an ailing system, it asks new questions. For example, in the health care system, besides trying to get enough money to build more hospitals and pay more doctors to care for the sick, it is asking, "What can we do to help people stay well?" This question is leading to "wellness clinics" that teach a person how to be well and not get sick. Well people don't need hospitals or doctors or high-priced technology.

Have our organizations really progressed toward wholeness, or only toward conflict, aggression, and war? I believe there has been progress with our organizations, even though it has been painful progress, with much war, aggression, and conflict. God will provide a way to utilize the present chaos and conflict to seek new alternatives creatively by asking different questions. This creativity in turn will enhance participation in the ongoing creation.

NORMATIVE DIRECTIONS

Many Christians hope that organizations will move toward transcending the subjective and objective philosophical foundations of the first (Western) and second (Communist) worlds while drawing upon other people's witness to the harmony in the ecology. What, then, should be the human agenda to prepare for the next step in the development of humankind? Perhaps the first task, mentioned above, is to deal with some of the most fundamental biblical images that have provided values for Christian life. The most crucial one that needs to be examined is the notion of hierarchy. Hierarchy is the original social sin— whether it be the hierarchy God, humankind, and lower animals; whether it be heaven, earth, and hell; whether it be sovereign, king, court, nobles, and peasant; or whether it be executive director, associate executive director, department head, and workers. People have tended to interpret all of creation in the fashion of hierarchical relationships rather than in an egalitarian, cooperative, or interdependent fashion with the understanding that each part makes a contribution to every other part and in return for that contribution receives its own livelihood. We have not yet understood that oppression is inherent in the very nature of hierarchy. Hierarchy puts one thing, one person, one animal over another. If a person who is at the top of a hierarchy is kind and patronizing, that situation is still oppressive. If the person who is at the top is directive and authoritarian, that situation oppresses more. Either way, hierarchy diminishes the quality of the human relationship. The same is true between governments and between businesses.

Only in a hierarchical system are power and self-interest important. To be sure, hierarchies can exist because many people are lazy—they would rather not think for themselves. They find it easier to follow orders. But that tendency too is related to original sin.

The biblical image of hierarchy is probably a misappropriation of the biblical intention. It may be that the Old Testament image of tribes, each with its own integrity interacting as equals to their mutual benefit, with a panel of "judges" to arbitrate disputes, represents the most creative biblical model. Only because of the sins of power and sloth did the Israelites opt for a lesser system, with a king.

Similarly, the prophetic message of persons of integrity interacting in right relationships for their common good is more creative as an image than is the "righteous" nations conquering their enemy in the name of God. Christians have tended to build images of relationship with one another, individually and corporately, more from the biblical models of the sins of people than from revolutionizing principles manifest in the prophets and in the teaching of Christ.

Christians—the prototype people, the living reminder of God's creative intention—are called to build new images, new dreams, based upon the central message of the

Bible. This task will require much more integrity, much more willingness to change, and much more willingness to be different than has normally been demonstrated. Without the difficult work of discerning the Spirit and building these renewed images, people will remain the captives of past sins.

Therefore I would guess that the norms by which Christians will judge images of progress in the future will have to do with questions like: Does the suggested option enhance hierarchy, or does it enhance a more egalitarian and qualitative style of relationship? Is it oppressive, or does it provide justice along with equal responsibility to each person and group in the society or the organization? Or, is it creative, in the sense that it heals, builds whole relationships, a sense of interdependence, ecological soundness, and the possibility for more effective participation in the creation?

So we must open ourselves anew to the possibility of transcending the present plateau in our development by better using conflict creatively and building qualitative interdependent relationships. Then our organizations will become redemptive and healing forces. We have used one illustrative biblical image of hierarchy as an example. However, we will need dozens of new and winsome images if we are to move beyond the present plateau into the new level of corporate creativity that we must have to be whole. As we pursue this new creativity we will begin to transcend what has been, and will begin to experience what can be. That is the task of every generation. It is the agenda for every congregation. It is the agenda for the church.

Appendix

SOME QUESTIONS FOR DISCUSSION

The material in this book is well suited for use by local church study groups. The following questions will help the reader and the group relate the content of each chapter to their own experiences in a developmental fashion.

Chapter I. COMMUNITY

1. What different kinds of organizations have you experienced?
2. What are the differences among these organizations?
3. Does the church, as organization, have any unique characteristics that make it qualitatively different from other organizations you know about?
4. What is the unique role of the congregation in forming the values of the community?
5. Should organizations in general, and congregations in particular, change? How do they change?

Chapter II. PURPOSE

1. Can you cite evidences that creation is in process?
2. What are some of the creative forces you have participated in or know about in your community?

3. What are some of the anticreative forces you observe, or even participate in, in your community?
4. Is the church in your community really qualitatively different from other community organizations? If not, why not? If it isn't, is it being faithful to its reason for being in the community?
5. Do you believe that the creation is moving toward fulfillment? Why?

Chapter III. TIME

1. Where do you believe your congregation is on the continuum?
2. From your experiences, what makes an organization creative or anticreative?
3. Do you know an organization that is especially good at helping its members grow into fulfilled and whole persons, while at the same time it is effective in contributing to a just community? Describe it.
4. In what ways do organizations you are part of oppress you?

Chapter IV. CHANGE

1. As you reflect on your own congregation, do you see it as reasonably balanced between its nurturing and outreach roles and its conserving and prophetic roles? If it is skewed, how? What are the results among your members or in the community?
2. Do you know illustrations where renewal has taken place in church or community organization? What was the impact on the people and the community?
3. Do you believe that God is at work among the organizations of your community? Do you think the church has any unique role to play among the organizations in your community? If so, what?

Chapter V. LIFE CYCLES

1. Are the roles that are being played by the lay leadership in your congregation primarily those of a growing organization or those of a declining organization?
2. Do you believe the growth or the decline of the community is more influential in the future of a congregation's life than the internal organizational dynamics? Why?
3. Do you know of times when your congregation has been more aggressive and times when it has been more passive?

Chapter VI. LEADERSHIP: ITS NATURE

1. Pick two or three of the most influential leaders you have known personally. What was their background—personal characteristics and training? How did they emerge as leaders? What was their style? Why did they impress you?
2. Do you believe it is possible for an organization to function in other than a win-lose manner?
3. Do you believe power is infinitely expandable? Why?

Chapter VII. LEADERSHIP: ITS FUNCTION

1. Do you know of some organizations where leadership is shared between the professionals and the laity in a creative way? If so, describe it. If not, what does that say about the creativity of organizations?
2. Is there any reason for congregations to develop new models for doing their work, as the congregation did that is described in this chapter? How do you think your pastor or ecclesiastical leaders (presbyter, superinten-

dent, associational minister, bishop) would react to such a radical departure from tradition?
3. Do you think there is any creative possibility in your community for neighboring churches to share ministerial specialties? Why?

Chapter VIII. FUTURE

1. Do you see signs of progress in your congregation and community? What are they?
2. Do you believe we as Christians have a prototype role to play?
3. What do you think might happen if we fail to fulfill the role that God has given us as the church? In your community? In our nation? In the world as a whole?